HAUNTED
LAKE TAHOE

HAUNTED LAKE TAHOE

JANICE OBERDING

Haunted
America

Published by Haunted America
A Division of The History Press
Charleston, SC 29403
www.historypress.net

CONTENTS

FOREWORD

"Her name is Janice; she is a good girl."—so well I remember this, her first story written while she was still a very small girl. The cadence of those words echoed in my ears while I tried to catnap before another grueling afternoon shift. Even then, I knew this girl was destined to become a writer, which indeed she has.

I'm proud of her as a daughter and especially proud of her writing. I know thorough research goes into everything she writes. From a very early age, Janice has explored every corner of Nevada. The Lake Tahoe area is one of her favorites. She loves Nevada and is well versed in its history.

I know that you will enjoy Janice's rendering of Tahoe and the area ghosts as they weave their way through one story after another. It seems they want to linger still, in various places, as several people have attested.

—Bonnie Harper

ACKNOWLEDGEMENTS

It takes a village to create a book. There are so many people I wish to acknowledge and thank for their help in this book (and other books as well). First, I thank my husband, Bill, for his willing participation in research, photography and whatever else I have needed along the way. Thanks goes to my mother (Mama), Bonnie Harper, for her encouragement and guidance and for writing the foreword to this book, and thanks to my sister Diane Grulke, a writer herself, whose suggestions are deeply appreciated. Thank you to my friend Cimarron Sam for his interesting experiences and stories. Thanks to Richard St. Clair for spending a beautiful spring day driving our friend Terri Hall-Peltier and me around the lake. Thanks to Richard Senate for sharing his notes on Truckee with me. Thanks to my friend Mona Hoppe for sharing her Truckee experiences and stories. Thanks to Terri Hall-Peltier for her friendship and help in all my book adventures and to Deborah Carr-Senger for her wit and friendship. Thank you to the many ghost investigators who have shared my enthusiasm for hunting ghosts over the years. Finally, there would be no book without a publisher's go ahead; I want to thank Artie Crisp and the people at The History Press for saying yes to my ideas and for bringing them to fruition.

INTRODUCTION

I'm often asked how I can believe that ghosts exist. This is usually followed by a look that says "you seem like a rational and reasonably intelligent person." Before anyone can answer a question about ghosts, there first has to be some agreement about what a ghost is. I've long believed that—and for the purpose of this book—ghosts are the essence (spirit) of someone who has died. It is not my intention to offer up proof of ghosts and hauntings; this would require someone with infinite patience and a deeper understanding of scientific matters than I myself possess. I have written this book with two purposes in mind: to tell the stories of ghosts that I and others have encountered at Lake Tahoe and to share some of the legends and myths that are an integral part of Lake Tahoe's history. Fans of the old television series *Bonanza* have seen Lake Tahoe in the opening scene of the show many times; that scene was filmed near Incline Village at North Lake Tahoe. Of course, the Cartwrights and their famous Ponderosa Ranch were fictional, but the breathtaking scenery is real—and it is haunted.

Ghosts are everywhere. But some places lend themselves to hauntings more than others. Lake Tahoe is such a place. The two-million-year-old lake does not entirely belong to California or Nevada. Instead, it straddles the borders of both states, thus giving California and Nevada equal, if at times contentious, regulatory rights over its shoreline. Since the near-pristine lake is an interstate waterway, Lake Tahoe is subject to the jurisdiction of the United States Coast Guard.

Lake Tahoe is 22 miles long; it is two-thirds in California and one-third in Nevada. It is the tenth-deepest lake in the world and the second-deepest lake in the United States, with a deepest point of 1,645 feet and a surface area of 193 square miles. There is enough water in the lake to cover the entire state of California to a depth of 14 inches. With thirty-nine trillion gallons, the lake contains enough water to provide everyone in the United States with seventy-five gallons of water per day for five years. The lake has its different areas, particularly North Shore and South Shore. If you plan to see the entire lake and its shoreline—and you must—keep in mind that the driving distance around the lake, from one end to the other, is about seventy-two miles. As you cover those miles, you will see the lake's color change from azure to turquoise and its surroundings change from tall pines, mountains and rustic, log-hewn buildings to high-rise hotels and casinos. Also in those miles, you will pass, albeit in the secluded distance, Tahoe's nude beaches; there are said to be seven of them, with Secret Cove and Secret Creek being the most popular. But this is a book about ghosts, so I'll just say that clothing is optional for the living and the ghosts at these locations.

Looking at the lake as an early morning mist shrouds its shoreline, it seems almost enchanted, and you can sense its haunted magic. Ghosts are more popular than ever, but ghostly legends and folklore have surrounded Lake Tahoe since long before Captain John C. Frémont discovered it on February 14, 1844. Of his first look at the lake, Frémont wrote in his journal:

> *Accompanied by Mr. Preuss, I ascended today the highest peak to the right from which we had a beautiful view of a mountain lake at our feet, about fifteen miles in length, and so nearly surrounded by mountains that we could not discover an outlet.*

Naturalist and environmentalist John Muir visited Lake Tahoe for the first time in October and November 1873. He called the lake the "queen of lakes." In his 1915 *Letters to a Friend*, a collection of letters he wrote to his friend Jeanne Carr, the following was written about Lake Tahoe on November 3, 1873:

> *Somehow I had no hopes of meeting you here. I could not hear you or see you, yet you shared all of my highest pleasures, as I sauntered through the piney woods, pausing countless times to absorb the blue glimpses of the lake, all so heavenly clean, so terrestrial yet so openly spiritual.—the soul of Indian summer is brooding this blue water, and it enters one's being as*

nothing else does. Tahoe is surely not one but many. As I curve around its heads and bays and look far out on its level sky fairly tinted and fading in pensive air, I am reminded of all the mountain lakes I ever knew, as if this were a kind of water heaven to which they all had come.

It is not surprising then that John Muir's ghost is said to haunt the Lake Tahoe region. According to author Charles A. Stenfield in his book *Haunted Southern California: Ghosts and Strange Phenomena of the Gold State*, the ghostly Muir, who appears in a greenish glow, has been known to point lost hikers in the right direction. If only all ghosts were this friendly. Alas, they are not, just as all lakes are not as captivating as Lake Tahoe.

Unlike other lakes, there are no outlets to the sea at Lake Tahoe. The lake's only outlet is the Truckee River, which flows east to Reno and then onward to Pyramid Lake. Some believe that beyond this connection there is also an underground connection that links Pyramid Lake with Lake Tahoe. Where there are legends and myths, there are ghosts. The Lake Tahoe area abounds in myths, legends and ghosts. Standing on land that is as ancient as the lake itself, the hotels and casinos on the South Shore dazzle with a twenty-first-century allure, but there is more here, much more. Lake Tahoe is truly one of Nevada's and California's treasures. Regardless of where you happen to be—Incline Village, South Lake Tahoe or anywhere in between—you can feel it. You can feel that this is a mystical place of mystery, magic and ghosts. After one visit, you will return again and again. That is the lure of Lake Tahoe. And it brings three million visitors to this area annually.

1
THE LAKE'S LEGENDS AND LORE

MARK TWAIN

Captain Frémont discovered the lake during his second expedition of the Great Basin. Frémont called the lake "Lake Bonpland" in honor of Jacques Alexander Bonpland, the noted French botanist who accompanied Baron Alexander von Humboldt on his exploration of the west. Charles Preuss, however, identified it as "Mountain Lake" on maps he later drew of the expedition. Thus began the confusion over what the lake should be called. Native Americans had been living on the shores around Lake Tahoe for hundreds of years before Fremont made his discovery. They called the lake "Tahoe," which is what many felt it should be called.

Others strongly disagreed; the debate raged for many years. In *Innocents Abroad*, Mark Twain, who did not like the name "Lake Tahoe," jumped into the fray with the following:

> *Sorrow and misfortune overtake the legislature that still from year to year permits Tahoe to retain its unmusical cognomen! Tahoe! It suggests no crystal waters, no picturesque shores, no sublimity. Tahoe for a sea in the clouds; a sea that has character, and asserts it in solemn calms, at times, at times in savage storms; a sea, whose royal seclusion is guarded by a cordon of sentinel peaks that lift their frosty fronts nine thousand feet above the level world; a sea whose every aspect is impressive, whose belongings are all beautiful, whose lonely majesty types the Deity!*

Tahoe means grasshoppers. It means grasshopper soup. It is Indian, and suggestive of Indians. They say it is Pi-ute—possibly it is Digger. I am satisfied it was named by the Diggers—those degraded savages who roast their dead relatives, then mix the human grease and ashes of bones with tar, and "gaum" it thick all over their heads and foreheads and ears, and go caterwauling about the hills and call it mourning. These are the gentry that named the Lake.

People say that Tahoe means "Silver Lake"—"Limpid Water"—"Falling Leaf." Bosh! It means grasshopper soup, the favorite dish of the Digger tribe—and of the Pi-utes as well. It isn't worthwhile, in these practical times, for people to talk about Indian poetry—there never was any in them—except in the Fennimore Cooper Indians. But they are an extinct tribe that never existed. I know the Noble Red Man. I have camped with the Indians; I have been on the warpath with them, taken part in the chase with them—for grasshoppers; helped them steal cattle; I have roamed with them, scalped them, had them for breakfast. I would gladly eat the whole race if I had a chance.

Certainly Mark Twain's words were of a different time, nonetheless they were thoughtless, cruel and derogatory. But everything evens out, eventually. There is an old saying, "What goes around comes around." In Mark Twain's case, this has proven true, although it would be over one hundred years in coming. There is a scenic cove on the lake that supporters recently wanted to name Samuel Clemens (Twain's real name) in his honor. Native Americans nixed the idea because of Twain's racist, derogatory comments about the Washoe and the Paiute tribes. The cove was not named after him.

During the winter of 1852, California's third governor, John Bigler, received word that a group of emigrants were stranded in the area. With the tragedy of the Donner Party still fresh in everyone's memory, he led a rescue party in to assist them. His actions were considered heroic, and soon afterward, the lake was unofficially renamed "Lake Bigler" in his honor. Despite the unpopularity of that name, largely due to Bigler's pro-Southern views during the Civil War, the California legislature passed an act in 1870 that officially legalized the name. In 1945, the legislature rescinded that act: "The lake known as Bigler shall hereinafter be known as Lake Tahoe."

Mark Twain often walked from Carson City to the lake, not a short stroll. Of his walk, he wrote:

We plodded on, two or three hours, and at last the Lake Burst upon us—a noble sheet of blue water lifted six thousand three hundred feet above the level of the sea, and walled in by a rim of snow-clad mountain peaks that towered aloft full three thousand feet higher still. It was a vast oval, and one would have to use up eighty or a hundred good miles in traveling around it. As it lay there with the shadows of the mountains brilliantly photographed upon its still surface I thought it must surely be the fairest picture the whole world affords!

And then there was that fire that Mark Twain and a friend were responsible for starting. He tells of that in *Roughing It*:

By and by our provisions began to run short, and we went back to the old camp and laid in a new supply. We were gone all day, and reached home again about night-fall, pretty tired and hungry. While Johnny was carrying the main bulk of the provisions up to our "house" for future use, I took the loaf of bread, some slices of bacon, and the coffee-pot, ashore, set them down by a tree, lit a fire, and went back to the boat to get the frying-pan.

While I was at this, I heard a shout from Johnny, and looking up I saw that my fire was galloping all over the premises! Johnny was on the other side of it. He had to run through the flames to get to the lake shore, and then we stood helpless and watched the devastation.

The ground was deeply carpeted with dry pine-needles, and the fire touched them off as if they were gunpowder. It was wonderful to see with what fierce speed the tall sheet of flame traveled! My coffee-pot was gone, and everything with it. In a minute and a half the fire seized upon a dense growth of dry manzanita chaparral six or eight feet high, and then the roaring and popping and crackling was something terrific. We were driven to the boat by the intense heat, and there we remained, spell-bound.

Within half an hour all before us was a tossing, blinding tempest of flame! It went surging up adjacent ridges—surmounted them and disappeared in the canons beyond—burst into view upon higher and farther ridges, presently—shed a grander illumination abroad, and dove again—flamed out again, directly, higher and still higher up the mountain-side—threw out skirmishing parties of fire here and there, and sent them trailing their crimson spirals away among remote ramparts and ribs and gorges, till as far as the eye could reach the lofty mountain-fronts were webbed as it were with a tangled network of red lava streams. Away across the water the crags and domes were lit with a ruddy glare, and the firmament above was a reflected hell!

Every feature of the spectacle was repeated in the glowing mirror of the lake! We sat absorbed and motionless through four long hours. We never thought of supper, and never felt fatigue. But at eleven o'clock the conflagration had traveled beyond our range of vision, and then darkness stole down upon the landscape again.

Mark Twain is not the only writer to have spent time at the lake. While working as a handyman at Lake Tahoe, Nobel Prize winner John Steinbeck not only met his first wife but also wrote his first novel, *Cup of Gold.* Long before Twain wrote Lake Tahoe's praises and hundreds of years before the rich and famous claimed the lake as their playground, the Washoe and the Paiute tribes lived on its shores and fished its clear waters. They referred to the lake as "Lake of the Sky" and told many stories concerning the lake and those who'd lived in the region long ago.

CAVE ROCK

Cave Rock is located on the southeastern shore of Lake Tahoe between Glenbrook and Zephyr Cove. Travel around the rock formation was treacherous and difficult until work began on the Cave Rock Tunnel on Highway 50, opened in 1931. Although it appears harmless, this is still a deadly section of roadway. Since the tunnel opened, there have been numerous automobile accidents, ending with fatalities, here. Climbers have also fallen to their deaths from the 360-foot-tall and 800-foot-wide Cave Rock, which is known as *De'ek Wadapush,* or "Rock Standing Gray," by the local Washoe people who have held De'ek Wadapush as a sacred place for centuries.

The Washoe believe Cave Rock is a place that should be respected by everyone and avoided by all but Washoe healers. At one time, the magnificent rock was a popular site with rock climbers. The Washoe tribe protested the fact that climbers were defacing the rock with their climbing implements. As you might expect, the climbers didn't want to give up their use of Cave Rock. But the Washoe pushed back. This was their holy place, and they didn't want it desecrated. The battle between the climbers and the Washoe went on for ten years. In 2008, the U.S. Forest Service finally decided to enforce a ban on climbing at Cave Rock.

Cave Rock from a boat launch site. *Photo by Bill Oberding.*

My Native American friend Cimarron Sam tells of two people who had hiked to the top of Cave Rock for sightseeing and photography:

> *One of the men sat on a rock while the other got his camera ready. He heard what sounded like a whooshing noise and looked up. The other man was gone. He had fallen to his death onto the rocks far below. There was no wind, it was as if someone had just pushed him from that rock.*

Beware the Water Babies

Water babies are blamed for the bodies of drowning victims that are never recovered from the depths of Lake Tahoe. But don't mention it. And whatever you do, don't speak aloud about water babies. Washoe legend has it that these tiny creatures are very powerful and can either be friend or enemy. And as enemies, they will drag you to a watery doom if you're not careful.

19

Water babies live in Pyramid Lake (north of Reno) and in the waters off Cave Rock. There is believed to be an underwater connection between these two bodies of waters. If you should be visiting this area of Lake Tahoe and hear what sounds like babies wailing, remember that this could well be the water babies' attempt to pull you in. These pitiful cries are how they coerce the unsuspecting into the water.

But what if someone wanted permission to go into the water to fish or swim? Early Washoe filled a basket with corn and pine nuts, sealed it with pitch and took it into the water as an offering. If it appeased the water babies, they were safe, if it didn't…

My friend Cimarron Sam remembers a childhood in which his grandmother would warn him and his siblings, "If you hear kids laughing and playing around the water, do not go down there."

Native Americans can't swim in Tahoe until someone drowns in the water that season. Yes, someone must drown each season. Cimarron told me it

A view of Emerald Bay, Lake Tahoe, California, during golden hour. *Photo by Frank Schulenburg.*

is because the water babies are looking for a soul. But it is not just in Lake Tahoe and Pyramid Lake that the water babies can be found. They are in all bodies of water.

VIKINGSHOLM

Located at the head of Emerald Bay is the former summer home of Lora Josephine Knight. The thirty-eight-room mansion was built in 1929. Today, tourists from around the world come to visit Vikingsholm, which is open for guided tours from early summer through early fall.

In the twentieth century, the Lake Tahoe area became a playground for the rich. A rush of wealthy people came to the lake, eager to build showcase summer homes, cottages and mansions on its shores. None of

them would build a more fabulous home than Lora Josephine Moore Knight's Vikingsholm.

Knight was an heiress with more money than she could spend in three lifetimes. And she liked things a certain way. No expense was spared in seeing that her summer home at the southwest end of Emerald Bay resembled a Scandinavian castle. Everything, down to the tiniest detail, was to be authentic. So she set off on a buying trip to Norway, Sweden and Finland with her architect and his wife. What couldn't be purchased would be expertly copied. The décor included six fireplaces of Scandinavian design, painted walls and ceilings and intricately woven carpets. A touch of whimsy was added with a carving of a woman whose face is a clock, and dragons were carved into two of the ceiling beams. According to folklore, the dragons would chase away evil spirits.

A generous woman, Knight opened Vikingsholm to friends and family and entertained them all summer long. Just for the fun of it, she would often take guests by motorboat over to Lake Tahoe's only island, Fannette Island, where they would be served tea in the stone teahouse that was built the same year as her mansion. Those houseguests who took excursions around the region returned to find that their hostess always had their cars cleaned and their gas tanks refilled after each outing. Knight's was a luxurious, carefree life, but sadly, she was only able to enjoy her fabulous summer home for sixteen summers.

Today, Vikingsholm and Fannette Island are overseen by the California Department of Parks and Recreation. Rumor is that both sites are haunted. We'll get to Fannette in a bit, but as for Vikingsholm, well, I have a theory.

Native Americans could not have been too happy with all these people rushing to an area they held dear and tearing down trees to build large homes. Thunderbird Lodge on the other side of the lake (we'll also get there later) is another such home that was built with a lot of money and little thought to preservation. Native Americans believe it is haunted. Couldn't it be the same at Vikingsholm?

HANK MONK

Listen! Do you hear the steady *clip-clop* of horses' hooves galloping across the wind? Could it be the ghostly Hank Monk driving his team across the mountain passes? Hank Monk was known in the Tahoe region as a stagecoach driver extraordinaire. His prowess with a team of horses became legendary throughout the country for the wild ride over the Sierras that he took newspaperman Horace Greeley on in 1859. As Greeley climbed into the coach, he made the mistake of telling Monk that he had a speaking engagement and was in a hurry to get to Placerville. Monk nodded his assent. He would get the man to his destination on time. The coach pulled out of Carson City at lightning speed and raced over the narrow mountain passes. Horace Greeley looking out the door became alarmed and urged Monk to slow down. Hank Monk, however, was not one to back down from a challenge or a promise.

"Keep your seat, Horace." He called down to his frightened passenger. "I'll get you there on time!"

Of his ride, Horace Greeley wrote, "Yet at this breakneck rate we were driven for not less than four hours or forty miles changing horses every ten or fifteen, and raising a cloud of dust through which it was difficult at times to see anything."

Monk did get his passenger to Placerville on time. And he couldn't wait to get to the nearest saloon and tell everyone within earshot all about Greeley's fear as the coach sped along the Tahoe shore. They all had a good laugh at Greeley's expense. Monk told a reporter, "I looked into the coach and there was Greeley, his bare head bobbing, sometimes on the back and then on the front of the seat, sometimes in the coach and then out, and then on the top and then on the bottom, holding on to whatever he could grab."

The tale spread across the country, and soon everyone was having a good laugh at Horace Greeley's expense. Thirteen years later, the story was still being told. Needless to say, this didn't make Greeley happy. Some said it was this story that ruined the former New York congressman's chances at defeating opponent Ulysses S. Grant in the 1872 presidential election.

Hank Monk is buried at Lone Mountain Cemetery in Carson City. When not behind a team of horses, Monk loved nothing more than partaking in a bottle of whiskey beside a warm fire. Monk's apparition has been seen at a local Carson City bar quietly guzzling his drink. And then there are those ghostly horse's hooves high up in the Sierras.

A MOTHER'S LOVE

An old Native American legend is the story of a young wife and mother who died suddenly, leaving an infant and her husband behind. The grieving husband dutifully spent the required four days and nights watching at her grave. During this time, he went without food or drink. On the fourth night, the grave suddenly opened, and the woman stepped out before him.

"Where is my child? Please give me my child," she demanded.

The husband did as he was told and quickly brought the baby to her. Without a word, he handed the child to her and watched in amazement as she took the child and nursed it. Then, holding the baby close in her arms, she turned and started to walk slowly away. Silently, he followed her. On and on they went, through the tall pines and out across the meadow.

Was he dreaming? He reached out to touch her, but she warned him off with a wave of her hand.

"Don't touch me." She said. "If you touch me, you must die too!"

She nursed the child once more and then placed it gently in her husband's arms. "Please go home now," she said, dissolving into air.

He did as he was told, but he was confused and uncertain. He wasn't quite sure if it had all been a dream brought on by his broken heart and hunger. When his perfectly healthy infant died a few days later, he received his answer. His wife had come back to get her baby. And because she had warned him to not touch her, he would live to be a very old man.

THE ONG

I wonder if this story isn't borne of memories of a prehistoric bird that once lived at Lake Tahoe. This Native American legend is that of the Ong, a monstrous bird that regularly rose out of the lake and greedily devoured any unlucky humans who happened to be nearby. Described as having the body of an eagle with webfeet and wings that were taller than the tallest pines; its hideous face was human like but covered with hard scales. The long's nest was located in the darkest depths of the center of the lake; the waters that rushed out of its nest filled the lake.

This evil creature was particularly fond of human flesh; the bodies of drowning victims in the lake were carried to its nest. But the Ong was

THE LAKE'S LEGENDS AND LORE

a coward that attacked only children, women or hunters who happened to be alone. Though no arrow could pierce its feathers and the strongest spear glanced off the scales of its face and legs, it lived in fear that someone would discover its weakness: it had no claws or beak.

Late one fall, the Washoes were making their final hunt before going to the valleys and leaving the lake locked in its blanket of winter snows. The chief's daughter was sixteen years old, marrying age. Custom decreed that she select the greatest hero in the tribe to be her husband. She was far more beautiful than any other maiden, and every man wished to make her his wife.

While everyone else enjoyed the festivities of an upcoming wedding, the young man who loved her was miserable; he was too young to go into battle with the other warriors and could not sit around the council fire with them. Now, someone else would claim his beloved. As he cursed the Great Spirit, the young man saw the Ong rising out of the lake. When the monstrous bird neared him, he jumped in the air to attract its attention.

Sure enough, the Ong swooped down and carried him away. A great cry of horror arose from those who watched on shore, but he was not afraid. The bird flew straight up into the sky until the lake and the forest and the mountains seemed small and distant. When it reached a great height, the Ong, as was its custom, dropped its prey into the lake and let the current draw it to its nest. But the young man had planned to outwit his adversary. He had attached a long buckskin cord first to his waist and then to the Ong's leg. When the bird opened its feet, the man did not fall. Furious, the Ong tried to grab him with its teeth. Each time the bird opened its mouth to bite him, the man hurled poisoned arrowheads down its throat.

Finally, the Ong fell into the lake and drowned. Thinking that her lover was dead, the chief's daughter, who had been watching from shore, was horrified. She paddled her canoe to where the bird had fallen, calling to her lover, "Tahoe! My darling, Tahoe!"

When the two of them floated ashore standing tall on the giant bird's wing, a roar of happiness arose from the crowd. It was decided then and there that Tahoe was the bravest of all the young men, and he would be the husband of the chief's daughter.

WHAT DID JACQUES COUSTEAU SEE?

This is one of those Tahoe myths that's been told and retold countless times. Most anyone at Tahoe can tell you about that. It seems everyone has his or her favorite version of the story. Some say it was a matter of national security and that the CIA was at Cousteau's doorstep demanding the evidence he discovered on the bottom of the lake. Others say it was sunken UFOs or prehistoric creatures that Cousteau saw.

So what did he see? The story involves oceanographer Jacques Cousteau and his trip to the bottom of Lake Tahoe in a submersible craft. Supposedly, Cousteau returned to the surface and proclaimed that the world wasn't ready for the horror he had just seen at the bottom of the lake. But what had he seen? Some people will tell you that Monsieur Cousteau saw nothing simply because he never visited Lake Tahoe. This makes sense to me. But wait a minute! His son Philippe did. And what did he see? Rumor has it that Lake Tahoe contains the bodies of drowning victims, as well as those of the unfortunate men who got on the wrong side of the mob and ended up swimming with the fishes. Then there are the bodies of Chinese railroad workers who also ended up in the depths of the frigid waters of both Donner Lake and Lake Tahoe. And all these bodies are supposed to be just there at the bottom of the lake, perfectly preserved after all these years.

In 1876, a former writer for the *Territorial Enterprise*, William Wright, who used the nom de plume Dan De Quille, published his *History of the Big Bonanza*. The book covered the Comstock, mining and some of Virginia City's more outlandish denizens. Wright, who wrote his book from memory, had not forgotten the beauty of Lake Tahoe: "No land can boast a more beautiful sheet of water than Lake Tahoe, and its surrounding form a fit setting for such a gem."

And then, after extolling the lake's virtues, Wright gave his readers the following reason why drowning victims were not recovered from Lake Tahoe:

> *It is not easy to swim in the waters of the lake. Owing to the great altitude and consequent decrease of atmospheric pressure, the water is much less dense than the water of a lake or stream at the level of the sea. On account of this lack of density and buoyancy, the bodies of persons drowned in the lake never rise to the surface. Many have been drowned in Lake Tahoe, but a body has never yet been recovered.*

Today, experts have an explanation why the bodies of drowning victims are not always recovered. They say the water's frigid temperatures, at its lower depths, play a part in keeping bodies so cold that decomposition doesn't set in. Thus, the gases that normally would be formed during the decomposition process are not present. Without the formation of these gases, a drowning victim's body may not rise to the surface. A slew of well-preserved bodies are what some guess Cousteau saw. It all sounds farfetched until we look at the next two stories.

A Scuba Diver

In his 1823 book *Don Juan*, Lord Byron says, "Truth is always strange, stranger than fiction." And so it is. The morning of July 10, 1994, promised to be just another hot summer day. A Reno city planner, forty-four-year-old Donald Christopher Windecker, and a friend set out for a dive near D.L. Bliss state park off the lake's west shore. It was a routine July day and a routine dive; all went as planned until the two men started to return to the surface from the one-hundred-foot depth. Suddenly, Windecker seemed to be having trouble with his equipment. As he began sinking, his friend attempted to help him. But he was low on air, and Windecker was rapidly descending. It was all happening so fast; there was nothing more he could do. Rescue divers searched the lake for hours, but they found nothing. The married father of two was just one more person who had vanished in the lake without a trace.

Almost seventeen years later to the day, a discovery was made off Rubicon Point. A diver found Donald Christopher Windecker's well-preserved body on an underwater shelf at a 265-foot depth. Still fully clad in diving gear and a 1994 certification on the scuba tank, the body was positively identified—using dental records. But wouldn't this tend to destroy the perfectly preserved theory?

Lee Taylor

Lee Taylor was a man with a dream. On November 13, 1980, the forty-five-year-old was at Lake Tahoe hoping to see that dream become a reality. Piloting the $2.5 million *Discovery II*, a forty-foot steel and aluminum craft powered by a sixteen-thousand-horsepower rocket, Taylor was out to break the world water speed record. Months before, he had tested the *Discovery* at

Walker Lake in central Nevada. But a more accessible location was sought, and Lake Tahoe it was.

To say that his sport was dangerous is an understatement. Nobody understood this better than Lee Taylor. He had cheated death twice before while piloting a speeding craft across the water; he knew the odds and accepted the danger. On the day of his run, weather conditions were not what Taylor and his crew had hoped for. He decided to go for it against the advice of his crew. Nearly one thousand spectators gathered on shore, along with Taylor's wife and child, to witness the record-breaking attempt.

The *Discovery* sped across the lake, attaining a speed of nearly three hundred miles per hour—then something went terribly wrong. The boat hit a wave, went hurling into the air and disintegrated. Although his helmet and other bits and pieces of the *Discovery* were located, Taylor's body would not be found until a week later.

TAHOE TESSIE

Scotland's Loch Ness is famous for its monster, Nessie. But there are monsters all around the world; not to be outdone, Lake Tahoe locals have dubbed their monster Tessie, or Tahoe Tessie. Stories of this creature, which is said to live in an underwater tunnel beneath Cave Rock, have been told by the Washoe and Paiute people for over a century. In that time, there have been numerous sightings of Tessie, and depending on whom you talk to, the monster is a large sea serpent, a big fish, "just a story" or a sea creature that somehow got lost.

Whatever Tessie is, the monster is a popular part of Lake Tahoe lore; according to some, evidence of Tessie has been suppressed in the name of tourism. In spite of this, Tessie still manages to make the news often enough to gladden the heart of any public relations person.

STRANGE DEATHS

When a ghost researcher hears about a ghost that no one can identify, it's a good idea to start looking into strange and unusual occurrences that might have given rise to a haunting. Here are two deaths that easily fit the category.

Captain Pomin

Lunchtime came and went with no sign of her husband, and Mrs. Pomin's concern grew. It was not like him to miss a meal. As Captain of the SS *Tahoe*, Ernest John Pomin prided himself on his punctuality. It was early December 1919; already a flurry of snow had blanketed the ground. As the minutes ticked by on the mantel clock, Mrs. Pomin's concern gave way to gnawing fear.

Finally, the anxious woman could wait no more. She contacted a group of her husband's friends who went to search for him in Tahoe City. It didn't take the men long to discover the captain's lifeless body lying in shallow water near the gangplank of his boat. Apparently, he had lost his footing and fallen, hitting his head on the edge of the boat. This was years before sophisticated forensic investigation techniques, so this was the explanation they accepted as fact. During the autopsy, no water was found in the elderly Pomin's lungs, so his death was ruled accidental.

The man who'd fearlessly piloted the SS *Tahoe* across waters fierce enough to frighten others off had died of a freak accident, just five days short of his seventy-first birthday. And he could well be the specter of an elderly man that haunts this area of Tahoe City.

SS Tahoe

Unless you're an advanced scuba diver. you probably won't be visiting the SS *Tahoe* anytime soon. You see, it rests in the lake at a depth of about four hundred feet in Glenbrook Bay.

The 169-foot boat was built in San Francisco and sent in pieces to Carson City by rail. From there, it was taken to Glenbrook, where it was assembled. The boat was launched with much fanfare in 1896 with Captain Ernest John Pomin at the helm. It would carry mail and tourists around the lake for the next thirty years.

With room for two hundred passengers, the SS *Tahoe* was elegance itself. Rich touches of mahogany paneling and Brussels carpeting were part of the décor throughout. Once known as the "Queen of the Lake," the old boat was famous in its time. But time moves on; eventually, the Queen of the Lake had served its purpose. It was not without its fans. When plans that called for the sinking of the SS *Tahoe* were announced, many people tried to save the boat, but its fate was sealed.

A steamer at a pier in Emerald Bay, Lake Tahoe, circa 1910. *Photo by Harold A. Parker. Library of Congress.*

Captain Pomin had been dead two decades when, on a warm August evening in 1940, just after the sun had slipped behind the Sierras, his beloved SS *Tahoe* was towed out and sunk off Deadman's Point at Glenbrook. Some claimed the boat was haunted and that they heard the distinct sounds of moaning and weeping emanating from the old boat as it slowly dropped beneath the water and into history.

In 2004, the SS *Tahoe* became the first maritime site in Nevada to be listed on the National Register of Historic Places. This would not have been possible without the work of a Reno diving group, New Millennium Dive Expeditions, which conducted record-breaking high-altitude dives to the boat in 2002.

Advanced scuba divers are welcome to explore. The rest of us will just have to be satisfied to look at photographs and to take divers' word whether any ghosts lurk on the SS *Tahoe*.

SONNY BONO

By any standard, Sonny Bono was a winner. In the 1960s, he and his wife, Cher, reached the pinnacle of the music industry with hits like "I Got You Babe" and "The Beat Goes On." Later, they starred in their successful weekly television show, *The Sonny and Cher Show*. After the pair divorced in the 1970s, Sonny became an actor and a politician. I know, I know, some might say that the two are one in the same. And perhaps they are, but not too many actors help pass laws. Sonny did. His most famous, and controversial, was the Copyright Term Extension Act named after him as the Sonny Bono Copyright Extension Act, which extended copyright terms in the United States. To detractors, the law is known as the Mickey Mouse Protection Act.

The man, who admitted to not voting until he was fifty-three years old, was elected mayor of Palm Springs and served from 1988 to 1992. When his congressional qualifications were questioned in 1992, Bono told a reporter for the *Los Angeles Times*:

> *What is qualified? What have I been qualified for in my life? I haven't been qualified to be a mayor. I'm not qualified to be a songwriter. I'm not qualified to be a TV producer. I'm not qualified to be a successful businessman. And so, I don't know what qualified means.*

In 1994, Republican Bono was elected to Congress and won reelection in 1996. In 1998, Sonny Bono; his wife, Mary; and their children were skiing in Heavenly Valley. While his wife and children headed down one slope, Bono took a different direction. His decision would prove fateful. As he sped through Orion, a heavily wooded area, he crashed into a tree and died there on the slope of massive head injuries.

And like they had with the deaths of so many other celebrities, the rumors started. Conspiracy, cover-up or murder—take your pick. Celebrities can't

South Shore of Lake Tahoe from the west. Heavenly Valley's ski runs can be seen quite clearly, as can just a bit of Job's Peak on the right. *Photo by Lara Farhadi.*

simply die like the rest of us and certainly not in freak accidents. Is Elvis Presley really dead? What about Tupac Shakur or Michael Jackson? Ever heard the story about John F. Kennedy not having been assassinated in Dallas? Alive and well, somewhere, it goes. If true, he'd be pushing the century mark and—you get the point.

Sonny Bono died at Heavenly Valley, that much we know. Does his ghost haunt that lonely section of Orion where his death occurred? Some claim he does. And they will tell you that they've seen him racing past them on the slopes only to vanish into thin air. But then there were also those stories of him haunting ex-wife Cher's Malibu home. And the beat—yes, it does go on.

Suicide and the Stars

Do you check your daily horoscope? Astrologer Aris J. Mack did, and he took it very seriously. Far worse than "the devil made me do it" and the homework-eating dog were the stars that told the astrologer to kill himself at Lake Tahoe. Or did they? The fault may not have been in the horoscope itself but in the interpretation. Surely, he's had some time to rethink that.

The June 5, 1931 edition of the *Mountain Democrat* reported:

> *Aris J. Mack 39, San Francisco astrologer, committed suicide by drowning in Lake Tahoe over the weekend "because the stars willed it."*
>
> *The man's body, dressed in a bathing suit, was found Monday near Lake Forrest. Under a pier nearby were his clothes, books on astrology and a note indicating that the suicide was something of an experiment. The note also asked that the body be buried on a hillside over-looking Lake Tahoe but Placer County authorities find this impossible because there is a state law requiring burials in cemeteries.*

If you're on the beach at Tahoe some evening and happen to see the glowing apparition of a man coming slowly toward you, think of Aris J. Mack and his astrology charts. You might ask him, "What sign are you?" or you might simply walk away.

THE DEATH OF CARRIE RICE

Who is the ghostly young woman that haunts the area around Shakespeare Rock? Some say she is Carrie Rice, who wasn't quite eighteen years old when she fell to her death from the famous rock one autumn afternoon in 1877.

On a cool September morning, Carrie Rice, William Cramer and several of their friends set out from Carson City to Glenbrook. The trip took a little over three hours; by the time they arrived in Glenbrook, the sun was high overhead. After a brief stop for refreshments, they headed toward Shakespeare Rock with its sweeping views.

When they reached their destination, they stopped and stared at the panoramic scene that lay before them. Here was the perfect vantage point. To go any further was foolhardy and dangerous. While the others lagged safely back, William Cramer clasped Carrie's hand in his. Laughing at their friends' trepidation, they started down a small path for an even better view. They were young. They didn't stop to think. Their shoes were not designed

Mount Tallac, Lake Tahoe Basin Management Unit, Lake Tahoe, Eldorado National Forest, California. *Photo by J. Cook Fisher.*

for such treacherous ground, and they started to slide, slowly at first and then the momentum pushed them onward toward certain death. Too late, they realized there was no place to go but down. As they tried desperately to grab hold of something that would stop their fall, Carrie gasped, "William, we are to die."

At the last possible moment, William Cramer managed to grab hold of a tree root; he survived. Carrie Rice did not. She tumbled down, down, down into the abyss. Her battered body was recovered a short time later

That sound isn't the wind whispering across treetops. It is Carrie Rice weeping, some claim. And her lonely apparition still walks the spot where she met her tragic death on that long-ago afternoon.

The Mysterious Disappearance of A. Childers

The restless spirit of A. Childers roams an area of Glenbrook. Some say he does this because he was murdered and wants the world to know it. He's not looking for justice, because the unhappy ghost long ago exacted revenge on his business partner who had too quickly forgotten him. Now, when someone vanishes without a trace, the prospect of foul play is usually considered. Using modern forensic methods, crime investigators can often solve even the most baffling puzzles. These methods of evidence analysis were virtually unheard of in the nineteenth century. Consequently, we are left to ponder ancient mysteries that will never be solved. One such mystery is the disappearance of A. Childers.

In 1874, J.A. Rigby and A. Childers came to Glenbrook with high hopes of profiting from the logging boom that was going on in the region. There were no trading posts or stores in the area. They had found their niche and decided to fill it—the men would open a store. Set on piles over deep water, the store quickly became popular with residents who welcomed the opportunity to purchase their goods closer to home.

The business flourished. Unfortunately, success was short and sweet for A. Childers. One morning, he disappeared without a trace. Rigby spent half the day looking for his missing partner. When he realized there was too much ground for one man to cover, he sought help. The search was as thorough as could be expected for the time. When neither a body or a living Childers were found, it was assumed the unfortunate man had missed his footing, fallen into the water and drowned the previous night.

The boardwalk and train at Lake Tahoe, California, circa 1908. *Photo by Geo. R. Lawrence Company. Library of Congress.*

After his partner vanished, the pragmatic Rigby took on two other partners and changed the name of the business. All went well, and the store continued to profit—until the building burned to cinders three years later. "The work of the ghostly Mr. Childers," some whispered. And perhaps it was.

2
GHOSTS AND HAUNTINGS

BILTMORE MARY

The gaming industry is unique. It is the lifeblood of Nevada, but it wasn't always legal. In 1931, Phil Tobin, a young assemblyman from Humboldt County, set out to change this when he introduced a bill to the Nevada legislature that would legalize gambling in the state. There were many in the Silver State who frowned on gaming. But Tobin's bill received wide support and moved quickly through the assembly and the senate. On March 19, 1931, Governor Fred Balzar signed the bill into law. Gambling had finally become a state-sanctioned reality for Nevada. Eventually, high-rise hotels and casinos would line the South Shore, and gambling revenue in these fabulous showplaces would far exceed that of the North Shore. But that was still many years in the future.

Now that Nevada had given the nod to gaming, astute businessmen and women were quick to realize what a draw legalized gambling could be. This was especially true at Crystal Bay on the North Shore of Lake Tahoe. Those with get-rich-quick dreams opened gambling halls for high rollers eager to tempt Lady Luck. Nevada and the North Shore were changed forever. Soon the famous and the infamous were rubbing shoulders in these picturesque establishments high in the Sierras. The Tahoe Biltmore was one of the early establishments at Crystal Bay. Its location was ideal for Bay Area residents who came to the lake for weekends of gaming and fun. As gaming succeeded

Above: Biltmore Hotel Casino. *Photo by Bill Oberding.*

Left: A sign at Biltmore Hotel. *Photo by Bill Oberding.*

at Lake Tahoe, those who owned gambling establishments in Reno took notice. In 1958, Lincoln Fitzgerald, owner of the Nevada Club in Reno, decided to expand. He purchased the Tahoe Biltmore and renamed it the Nevada Lodge.

Under Fitzgerald's direction the Nevada Lodge became one of the most popular places at the lake. The building was remodeled and enlarged. With the addition of a new showroom, it was suddenly necessary to provide exciting entertainment. *Vive les Girls* was the answer. The show was a French revue that featured nude and scantily clad gorgeous young women. As you might expect, it was a hit. For the next few years, customers flocked to see *Vive les Girls*, which was featured in the Topaz Room at the Nevada Lodge.

When Lincoln Fitzgerald died in 1981, his Nevada Lodge was sold. The new owners changed the name back to the Tahoe Biltmore. Gone forever was the Topaz Room, and *Vive les Girls* was just a memory. The ghost of one dancer, however, is said to remain on the premises.

As part of their orientation, new employees at the Biltmore are told about the ghost of Mary. The ghostly Biltmore Mary is said to have been a dancer in the *Vive les Girls* revue. Her lover is believed to have been a married man who held a management position at the Nevada Lodge.

One rainy night, Mary and her lover had a terrible fight. Cruel words were hurled back and forth. Finally, he admitted that he had no intentions of leaving his wife and stomped out the door. Mary was heartbroken and spent the next few hours consoling herself at the bar. What happened next is shrouded in mystery and speculation.

There are several stories about how the beautiful showgirl met her fate. One has Mary going back to her room and committing suicide with sleeping pills. Another has the distraught young woman jumping in her car and speeding down icy Mount Rose Highway. Halfway down the hairpin curve, she lost control of her car and was killed when it crashed into boulders far below.

Regardless of how Mary died, one thing many people agree on is that she is still at the Biltmore. Part of the showroom where she performed has been converted into a wedding chapel. She makes her presence known with an occasional flicker of the lights and a wispy cold breeze. Another of her favorite spots is an area backstage where she's been known to move things around or play with the lights.

Although no one has actually seen Mary, many have felt her presence. While doing filming for a television special at the Cal Neva, I met a man who had once worked at the Biltmore. Darien, as I will call him, had been told several stories of the ghostly Mary by his co-workers. Being the skeptical sort, he'd decided Mary was nothing but the product of overworked imaginations.

A late-night experience changed his mind. It was the middle of winter. Winds were howling across the Sierras, and snow blanketed the streets and the parking lot. The casino was empty except for a few employees and the regular customers who came regardless of the weather.

Darien took his dinner break and, being new to snow country, stepped outside just long enough to see how much snow covered his truck. When he came back into the building, he had the distinct feeling of being followed. As he made his way down the hall, he turned to see who was walking so closely behind him. To his amazement, there was no one there. More than a little surprised to be alone in the hall, he heard the sound of a woman's laughter. The laughter, he noticed, seemed to grow louder as he walked across the deserted stage area. Suddenly, an icy chill enveloped him, and he felt someone tap him on the shoulder. He spun around expecting to see a co-worker. No one was in the area but him.

"OK," he said aloud. "I know that you're really here, Mary."

It was the last he heard or saw of the ghostly Mary, but the incident was enough to convince him of her existence.

Perhaps Biltmore Mary simply craves attention and acknowledgement. One woman remembers giggling at the story of the ghostly Mary when she first went to work in the offices of the Tahoe Biltmore.

> *I'm very organized, what some people call a real neat freak. You know, there is a place for everything, and everything in its place. That's how I work; my desk is always in order.*
>
> *Every time someone would blame Mary for something, I actually laughed out loud. I mean, here they were, a group of adults, blaming a ghost for misplacing their phonebooks and whatever else was lost.*
>
> *One morning, I wasn't feeling very well, and I snapped at a co-worker when she blamed Mary for losing an important file.*
>
> *"For Heaven's sake! Why don't you just admit you misplaced the file and be done with it?"*
>
> *"I know where I put the file, and it's not there!" she said.*
>
> *"Come on! We both know that gobbledygook ghost stuff is for kids. And frankly, I'm getting tired of hearing about Mary."*
>
> *Apparently that didn't please Mary. The next morning, my desk was in such a state of disarray it took me over an hour to clean it. Every afternoon I left a neat desk, but in the morning, it was always the same—a wreck.*

The office door was locked, and we all left at the same time; yet my desk was being messed up like you wouldn't believe.

Finally, the gal that I'd snapped at told me it was probably Mary wanting me to acknowledge her.

At that point, I was ready to try anything. "What the heck," I laughed. "Mary, I acknowledge you, now please don't mess up my desk anymore."

From then on, my desk was exactly as I left it the night before.

GHOSTS OF THE CAL NEVA LODGE

At this writing, the once fabulous Cal Neva Lodge that sat amid tall pine trees and enormous granite boulders is closed for remodeling. Big plans are in the works. When it reopens, the Cal Neva will be vastly different from the place that Frank Sinatra knew so well. Old Blue Eyes might even have trouble recognizing his beloved place. His specially built heliport will be history. The swimming pool where the ghostly Marilyn Monroe occasionally takes a dip will be elsewhere.

You can catch a breathtaking view of the lake from almost anywhere on the property. This was part of the rustic charm that kept many Hollywood notables coming back to the Cal Neva at Crystal Bay again and again. Back in the day, the Cal Neva was the place to rub shoulders with the stars, like silent film star Clara Bow, who lost a whopping (and it was back in the day) $13,000 playing blackjack in the casino. It was an action-filled place where the coolest of the cool hung out. Judy Garland was discovered at the Cal Neva. Parts of the 1930 film *Lightnin'*, starring Will Rogers and Marie Dressler, were filmed here. But there was a dark and sinister side as well. Rumors persist about the waters at the Cal Neva being a convenient body dump for hit men who had cadavers to dispose of.

A succession of owners has tried to keep the Cal Neva viable in a tourist market that has seen tremendous change since the days when Frank Sinatra and the Rat Pack ruled. None have really succeeded. It's been this way since Robert Sherman built that log cabin in 1926. This leads to a belief that the Cal Neva is cursed and that some of those who've been connected to it have not come away unscathed.

Rumor was that long before Frank Sinatra decided to purchase the Cal Neva, he came here brokenhearted when sultry actress Ava Gardner dumped him in 1951. In a pitiful ploy to win her back, he slit his wrists. Luckily for

The Cal Neva Lodge. *Photo by Don Graham.*

him, he didn't die. But Ava still didn't want him. She was done with the romance, and she moved on. Eventually, he would, too.

The Cal Neva had always been a special place for Sinatra when he decided to buy it in the early 1960s. The decision focused worldwide attention on the singer and the Cal Neva. His dreams loomed large. He envisioned turning the lodge into one of the most spectacular spots on the North Shore. Certainly it was a business venture, but he probably also wanted a place where he his friends and members of his Rat Pack could come and get away from it all. Peter Lawford, Joey Bishop, Sammy Davis Jr. and Dean Martin had spent plenty of time with Sinatra at the Sands in Las Vegas. Now, he would own a piece of property with a spectacular view of the lake. Sinatra had gained fame, wealth and women. Could anyone ask for more? When the dust settled, the new showroom rivaled most of those in both Las Vegas and Reno. Sinatra proudly appeared on stage in the new room and offered other top-name entertainers as well. Ella Fitzgerald, Dean Martin, Tony Bennett and Lena Horne were among those who appeared at Frank Sinatra's Cal Neva Lodge.

Some members of John F. Kennedy's family were regulars at the Cal Neva and awaited the 1960 presidential election results in one of its pine-enshrouded cabins. In addition to the powerful movers and shakers of the day, Frank's pals and acquaintances were always welcome at the lodge. To make it easier on them, a heliport was built on top of the building for fast entrances and exits.

Marilyn Monroe was one of Sinatra's friends who came to visit as often as possible. In 1960, she was in Reno filming *The Misfits*. During that time, she and her husband, Arthur Miller, drove up to the Cal Neva, where Frank entertained them and other members of the cast. And the ghosts linger.

Sinatra, Monroe and a bodyguard of mobster Sam Giancana are all known to haunt certain areas of the Cal Neva property. Monroe is the ghost who is most often spotted. Not content to stay in one location, she has been seen roaming the hallways, the tunnel, the parking lot and her former cabin.

Ghost Along the Highway

Highway 28 is an old road. It was used in the timber industry as far back as the 1880s. Paved in 1932, the highway has changed little since the late 1940s. Fans of the old *Bonanza* television series might remember it as the location of the Ponderosa. Think about this if you are driving along the highway late at night and should happen to see a man on the side of the roadway. Did you notice that he seems to be disoriented and that he vanished before you could get a good look at him? You've probably seen the ghost of Highway 28. But he's not the only specter to haunt these highways. Like the others, his identity is unknown. Here's where the ghost investigator steps in. While numerous deaths and tragedies have happened on the roadways around Lake Tahoe, there is reason to believe this ghost is that of Richard Anderson, a deputy who died while driving here back in 1962.

Anderson's beautiful, young wife, according to one story, was a former girlfriend of Frank Sinatra's. Another says it wasn't until she went to work at the Cal Neva that she caught Sinatra's eye. Either way, she was now happily married to the deputy and wanted nothing to do with Sinatra, his fame or his money. What's more, she told him this. Sinatra was not happy; he did not like being told no. He was used to having things his way. So he began making rude, suggestive remarks to her whenever he ran into her. When Anderson

Lake Tahoe in the fog. *Photo by Bill Oberding.*

heard about this, he was furious, but he waited until he was at the Cal Neva one night to pick up his wife. When he saw Sinatra, Anderson ran up to him and said, "Leave my wife alone."

Embarrassed and probably intimidated by the towering Anderson, Sinatra apologized and agreed to stop pestering Mrs. Anderson. That should have been the end of it. It wasn't. A week later, Anderson came to pick up his wife and went to the kitchen to talk with a friend. Sinatra came charging in demanding, "What the —— are you doing here?"

While Anderson tried to explain, Sinatra caught him unawares and hit him. And that was a mistake. Anderson returned the punch, hitting Sinatra so hard that he bloodied his nose, leaving him unable to perform in the showroom for a week. That really should have been the end of it, but it wasn't.

Two weeks later, on the night of July 17, 1962, Anderson and his wife were driving on Highway 28 near the Cal Neva when a maroon convertible came out of nowhere, rushing up behind them and forcing them off the road. Anderson lost control of the car and was killed instantly when his

Above: A view of Lake Tahoe. *Photo by Bill Oberding.*

Below: A view of Lake Tahoe from the highway. *Photo by Bill Oberding.*

car slammed into a tree. Mrs. Anderson was thrown from the car and suffered severe injuries. Who drove the convertible? Was it a drunk driver, an inexperienced driver showing off to friends or someone Sinatra sent to get even with Anderson? That's something we will never know. What we do know is that Anderson's parents remained convinced that Sinatra was behind the death of their son.

Marilyn Monroe Slept Here

The week prior to her death, Marilyn Monroe sought solace at the Cal Neva. At thirty-six years of age, her life was falling apart. She was a star whose dazzle was fast fading. Notorious for being late on the set, she was fired from her latest film, *Something's Got to Give*. For the first time in her life, her career didn't seem so promising. As she faced uncertainty, she might have wondered what the future held for her. By Hollywood standards, she was on the wrong side of thirty. Forty was a few short years away, and just as gossips predicted, her marriage to Arthur Miller had finally crumbled. When he met Inge Morath, a photographer, on the set of *The Misfits*, it was all over. That had to be hard on the ego.

Whatever her relationship had been with the Kennedys, it was over. Monroe was suddenly a persona non grata with both the president and his brother, the attorney general. Desperate for an explanation, she made continual phone calls to both men; none were returned. According to some, she spent the last days of her life in a drug-induced stupor, alone in the cabin Frank Sinatra had assigned to her.

A rumor that has persisted for many years concerns Monroe's near overdose less than a week before her actual death. After personnel discovered her in a near comatose state, she was revived, taken through the Cal Neva's secret underground tunnel and driven to Reno. There, she boarded a private plane and was flown back to Los Angeles and her fate.

Is the cabin still haunted by the restless spirit of the beautiful blond movie star? Marilyn Monroe sightings have been reported at other places—including Hollywood, Los Angeles and Reno. Nonetheless, there are people who regularly went to stay in this cabin so that they could communicate with the spirit of Monroe. She is, they say, quite content to stay on at the Cal Neva indefinitely. This might seem strange in light of the desperation of her last days at Lake Tahoe, but some of her happiest times were spent here as well. Some psychics who've contacted Monroe at the cabin have also said that her only regret is that she wishes she would have received more respect in life than she did.

Monroe's cabin is rustic and small by today's standards, but there is that million-dollar view of the lake and surrounding mountains and, of course, Monroe's presence. She slept in a special round bed in the cabin, but it's long gone. It was removed years ago because hotel staff realized that people were taking pieces of it home as souvenirs.

The décor in the cabin has been changed several times since Monroe stayed here; nonetheless, there is a sense of awe the first time you walk through the door. A star slept and dreamed and made plans that never came to be here. It's been more than fifty years since her death, and she still captivates us, evidenced by the success of the film *My Weekend with Marilyn*.

Did Robert Kennedy share this cabin with Monroe in happier times? If not him, then who? What thoughts ran through her mind as she gazed out at the beauty of Lake Tahoe? Was she so distraught during the last weeks of her life that she didn't even notice the spectacular view afforded her? Did she plot the unhappy end to her short life here in this cabin? No one knows. But we do know that Marilyn Monroe slept here.

Marilyn, Do You Hear Us?

Her name is still magic; she is as sought after in death as she was in life. There was no question that for a paranormal conference presented by Truckee Meadows Community College, one of the activities would be a ghost hunt in Marilyn Monroe's cabin at the Cal Neva. On the night of the event, attendees eagerly lined up to take turns trying to contact the dead celebrity in the small cabin. Psychics and investigators using dowsing rods, cameras and audio recorders called to Monroe in the great beyond. They wanted a sign, any sign that she was paying attention and that the grave is not the end. A psychic informed the group that Monroe was present and delighted to see so many fans in her cabin. She twirled around and added, "Marilyn is so excited to have you all here, and she is dancing."

My friend Terri Hall-Peltier was wearing a lovely rhinestone brooch that had once belonged to her mother. One of the psychics claimed the brooch had enchanted the ghostly Monroe, who, it just so happened, was in the cabin with us at that moment.

Terri eagerly asked, "Marilyn, did you know my mother?"

To her surprise, she received a very distinct Class A EVP (electronic voice phenomena, which some believe to be the recorded voices of the dead) that answered in the affirmative. (While a lot of EVP is garbled and indistinguishable, Class A is the best and most easily understood EVP attainable.) Did she know my friend's mother? It's highly unlikely. Perhaps this wasn't even the ghostly Marilyn Monroe responding to our questions; but then again, maybe it was.

While we communicated with the spirits, another friend, Rod Smith, stepped into the bathroom with his new digital camera. What the heck? He took a photograph in total darkness hoping to capture something, anything. The resulting photo strongly resembles the face of Marilyn Monroe.

Other Marilyn Sightings

A young Monroe fan told me the following incident:

> I've always adored Marilyn Monroe. For me, there was never any other place to get married but the Cal Neva. The only reason we spent our honeymoon in the newer high-rise hotel was because Marilyn's cabin wasn't available at the time.
>
> One evening as we were dressing for dinner, I said, "I think this room is haunted."
>
> He didn't believe in ghosts or hauntings and laughed uproariously at me. Suddenly, a look of fright crossed his face.
>
> "What's wrong?" I asked him.
>
> "Something just brushed against my neck, then rapped me on the back of the head," he said.
>
> At first, I thought he was teasing with me. His demeanor convinced me he wasn't.
>
> "Make it stop," he begged.
>
> "Marilyn, or whoever you are, please stop. You're frightening my husband."
>
> His face relaxed, and he whispered, "Thanks honey."
>
> Later that night as we were drifting off to sleep, he whispered, "I will never tease you about ghosts again, honey. I promise."

In Frank's Cabin

Psychics who've spent any time in Frank's Sinatra's cabin at the Cal Neva believe his spirit is there. He spends time throughout the lodge. Friends and I were hoping to prove this one night in October years ago. News reporters love ghost hunters, especially at Halloween, when the world says maybe they're on to something and news directors will do anything to get a story. Halloween was mere days away, and ghost-hunting friends and I were at the Cal Neva Lodge with a local news crew. We stepped into Frank Sinatra's cabin and talked of the secret tunnel that led to Frank's closet and of who might have used that tunnel to come into this cabin unseen.

Then, we discussed Sinatra and why he might be hanging on, even in the hereafter. We extolled the virtue of being respectful to the spirits while the cameraman trained his camera on us and not on the remote control lying on a nearby desk. To our amazement, the remote control rose into the air and did a complete 360-degree turn before gently returning to the desk. Was it the ghost of Frank Sinatra? We like to think it was. But that's not the point. The camera didn't catch the event. We saw it, and we know what happened. It was a shared personal experience that we can talk, wonder and write about forever. Ghost investigators call this anecdotal evidence. And it is only proof in so much as you believe what I've told you.

In the Frank Sinatra Celebrity Showroom

With the Sinatra name on the Cal Neva Lodge, it prospered. Movie star magic was in the air. Frank and the Rat Pack were all known to hang out here from time to time. But Sinatra was a singer, and one of the first things he did was have the showroom remodeled. He wanted it acoustically perfect. And it was. In a room that seats two hundred or more, it is possible to stand on the stage and be heard without using a microphone. I've tested this out and it is true.

Ghost-hunting friends who accompanied me to the Cal Neva one afternoon were convinced that Sinatra was still in his showroom when one of them felt a ghostly hand pat her on the leg. While we attempted to record EVP, we chatted away to, we assumed, the ghost of Sinatra. We received no answers to our questions and no proof—other than that hand, of course. Later, when we talked to employees about it, some admitted that they, too, had felt Sinatra's presence in the showroom. One young lady told us that once she was alone in the showroom and had started to sing an old Sinatra tune. Suddenly, she felt a hand slapped across her shoulder—not friendly and not menacing, just enough to let her know that the ghostly Sinatra wasn't pleased with her singing. From here on out, she would not sing while working in the showroom.

"Offending Frank is the last thing anyone here wants to do," she admitted.

Occasionally, the sound of laughter drifts through the empty showroom. Equipment has been known to quit working for no apparent reason. This was especially true when someone had the audacity to question the ghost stories. Don't doubt the presence of Frank. To do so may bring down more than the doubter bargained for, according to some employees. During a late-afternoon rehearsal, a member of the group that was performing in the showroom decided to make light of the ghostly Frank and Monroe.

No sooner had he announced that ghost sightings were just overworked imaginations than all of the equipment stopped working. After an hour of trying to find the source of the problem, they gave up; there was nothing more for them to do but leave the stage. It was the last time they joked about the ghosts at the Cal Neva.

The showroom light booth is also the site of ghostly activity, say some employees. A former lighting technician is thought to be responsible for items being moved or misplaced in the booth. Only a few employees ever had the key to the light booth, which was kept locked. One employee told the following story:

> I am always careful to turn the lights off when I leave for the night. I've worked here a long time, and it's a habit. But the day I came in and found the lights on, I knew the stories about a ghost in the light booth were true. Only a couple of us even have keys to the door, so I asked who went into the booth after I left. No one had.

Another employee said that one night, she had watched as a heavy door in the light booth, which can barely be pushed open with both hands, slowly opened of its own volition. While she was trying to figure out how the door had opened, it closed with a bang and startled her.

Frank in Charge

With Frank Sinatra in charge, it was well known that the Cal Neva was where the stars played. As the lodge's popularity soared, rumors surfaced concerning Sinatra's plans to open a fabulous nightclub in Reno, fifty-five miles south. The plans called for guests to be shuttled back and forth via helicopters. After all, Sinatra had a heliport on top of the Cal Neva. This never came to fruition. Barely a year after Monroe's death, Frank Sinatra's ownership of the Cal Neva was rapidly coming to an end.

When the Nevada Gaming Commission implemented its black book, mobster Sam Giancana's name was listed among those undesirables who were never permitted entrance into Nevada gambling establishments under any circumstances. If Frank Sinatra was aware of this rule and of the black book, he chose to ignore it.

Love makes the world go round. But infatuation brought Sinatra's reign at the Cal Neva down. In July 1963, mobster Sam Giancana was seeing Phyllis McGuire, a member of the McGuire Sisters singing group. The McGuire Sisters were a popular trio with number-one hits like "Sugar Time" and "Sincerely." They were booked at the Cal Neva for an appearance in the showroom that July. This is where Sinatra's trouble started. When Sam Giancana discovered that the McGuire Sisters were at the Cal Neva, the besotted gangster decided to visit his love. Nothing was going to stop him.

Four years earlier, he had used the alias S. Flood and checked into Wilbur Clark's Desert Inn in Las Vegas, only to be served with a subpoena to appear before the Senate select committee on the improper activities in the labor or management field in Washington, D.C. The memory of that incident wasn't enough to keep him from Phyllis. Noted for his loyalty to his friends, Sinatra, according to some sources, not only gave Giancana access to the Cal Neva but also allowed him to stay in one of the cabins. So while Sam Giancana partied it up with Phyllis McGuire at the Cal Neva, the FBI combed the countryside in search of him. When they found out he was at the Cal Neva, no one was amused, leastwise the Nevada Gaming Commission.

On August 29, 1963, Edward A. Olsen, chairman of the Nevada Gaming Commission, received a phone call from an employee who informed him that Sinatra was upset at publicity concerning the commission's investigation into Giancana's presence at the Cal Neva. Apparently, word had leaked to the media concerning the investigation of the Cal Neva's direct violation of gaming commission rules. Like it or not, Sinatra had some explaining to do. Two days later, a furious Sinatra called Olsen himself. The first thing he wanted to know was why Olsen wouldn't come to the Cal Neva and meet with him. When he was told that wasn't going to happen, Sinatra, true to form, yelled that Olsen was acting like "a —— cop." Throughout the conversation, Sinatra's speech was accentuated by a barrage of four-letter words, ones that are, incidentally, still considered too vulgar for television viewing audiences, even by today's relaxed standards.

"Listen, Ed, I haven't had to take this kind of —— from anybody in the country, and I'm not going to take it from you people…I want you to come up here and have dinner with me!" Sinatra demanded.

Olsen refused.

Sinatra was a star and, thus, accustomed to getting his own way. He ranted and raved, but this was one fight he couldn't win. For his blatant disregard of the gaming commission's regulations, Sinatra's license was revoked after a hearing. Not only was he forced to give up ownership of the Cal Neva, but he also had to give up the shares he owned in the Sands in Las Vegas. It must have been a crushing blow to the singer. He'd worked so hard to make the Cal Neva his showplace, only to meet his match with the Nevada Gaming Commission. It has been more than fifty years since Frank Sinatra owned the Cal Neva, but he is not forgotten here. The showroom bears his name, the hallway walls outside the showroom are lined with black-and-white photographs of him and his piano is center stage. It's not surprising that the showroom and the backstage area are most often associated with Sinatra sightings or hauntings.

In the backstage area where mobster Sam Giancana reportedly sat, hidden from view and watching his girlfriend, Phyllis McGuire, perform, a man's presence is usually sensed. During an investigation of the backstage area, a sensitive felt the presence of someone who "hadn't been very nice in life—someone a little rough around the edges." Those involved in the investigation assumed this was either Sam Giancana or one of his bodyguards.

Shortly after the arrival of Frank Sinatra's piano, a strange incident occurred. A large photo of the singer in his prime was displayed. One night, the photo mysteriously vanished and has never been found. The ghostly Sinatra is also said to be responsible for the late-night piano music that is sometimes heard coming from the darkened showroom. Many Cal Neva employees tell of ghostly encounters with the singer they adoringly refer to as "Frank." One person tells of seeing a tall figure he believes was Frank sauntering across the stage. "Like he was singing or entertaining an audience," he explains.

A young woman who has been brushed against by an unseen presence in the showroom several times knows it was the spirit of Frank Sinatra. She said, "He's returned here because he loved this place so much!" Smiling, this woman, who wasn't born until years after Sinatra lost ownership, smugly added, "And no one can kick him out of here this time around!"

Sinatra did sing a song about how wonderful love was the second time around. Perhaps he feels the same in regards his ownership of the Cal Neva.

Séance in the Showroom

Many people are against séances because they believe that they open a portal to the next world. Yet these same people think nothing of taking cameras, recorders and other devices into haunted locations and asking the spirits to interact. To me, it is the same exact thing. Regardless of what method you use, if you ask spirits to interact with you, you are opening a portal.

Several years ago, friends and I were working on an episode of the British television show *Dead Famous* that was being filmed at the Cal Neva. As part of the show, a séance was held on the stage of the Frank Sinatra Celebrity Showroom. My friends, who are both spirit mediums, led the séance.

As an observer, it was my responsibility to see that there was nothing fake going on. I thoroughly checked under and around the table and then took my spot off camera to watch the proceeding. The participants settled around the table and gazed at the flickering candlelight that cast shadows across each of their faces. The showroom was eerily silent as the psychic who would channel called softly for the spirits of Frank Sinatra, other Rat Pack members and Marilyn Monroe to join us.

Minutes passed. While seemingly in a trance, the psychic began speaking in a language that sounded like it might have been a Native American dialect. None of us understood the words, but their anger and intensity were undeniable. Then, he said the word *mataba* several times. Thanks to Filipino friends, I knew that *mataba* means "fat" in Tagalog. Now, I wondered if he might have been speaking in Tagalog all along. Before I could remember other words he'd said, another spirit appeared to take possession of the psychic.

Unaccustomed to channeling during séances, the psychic became extremely agitated as several spirits attempted to speak through him at once. He jumped up, dropped back on the chair and banged his head on the table. The mediums tried to help him by calmly talking him through the incident.

While they did this, another participant suddenly jumped up and yelled in a loud deep voice, "Get out!"

Later, he would say that he didn't know what had come over him. He had no idea what, or who, had caused him to do this. Silent for a moment, the psychic began to speak rapidly in a different voice. When asked who he was, the spirit refused to identify itself.

"His mannerisms and voice were those of Sammy Davis Jr.," someone suggested after the séance.

"He was part of the Rat Pack," another person agreed.

The participants then called to Sinatra and Monroe. However, neither the ghostly Frank Sinatra nor Marilyn Monroe chose to make an appearance at the séance. Perhaps they had more important engagements that night.

Showroom Photograph

We all want evidence—proof, if you will—that ghosts aren't merely the stuff of imagination, that they exist. To that end, we use equipment to capture photographic and auditory evidence. When an amazing photograph of a ghostly presence surfaced a few years ago, everyone wondered about it. Shot in the showroom, the photo captivated those who saw it. All agreed that it was one of the best ghost photographs ever taken. But there was something decidedly negative about that shot. A feeling you had whenever you looked at it too long. Was it the ghostly person in the shot or a pervading sense of doom?

Aside from that, there is always the question is it a fake? Anything as good as that photograph would seem to have been manipulated, Photoshopped or otherwise doctored.

What did the photographer have to say about his photo? We will never know this. A few weeks after taking the photograph, the photographer committed suicide.

The Tunnel

What would the Cal Neva be without a tunnel? Many people feel that the tunnel is the most haunted spot on the property. Marilyn Monroe was believed to have left the Cal Neva by way of the tunnel on her last visit here. Rumor is that both John Kennedy and, later, Robert Kennedy sneaked through the tunnel for clandestine visits in Monroe's cabin. Mobster Sam Giancana is said to have used the tunnel when he came visiting.

I spoke with an employee who told me that he has been alone in the tunnel many times. Each time he has had the same distinct feeling of being watched. "I've never seen a ghost or anything in the tunnel, but I know it's haunted just the same," he said.

An actress who portrayed Marilyn Monroe on a television special said she felt there was a friendly presence with her the entire time she was in the tunnel. She believes it was Marilyn herself and that she was letting her know she approved her impersonation. Others have contacted Monroe in the tunnel, but she is sometimes morose, especially when she is the only ghost present. Those who associate orbs with ghostly activity usually capture several orbs in the tunnel. Some of these, they say, are Marilyn Monroe and Frank Sinatra.

The tunnel was most likely built to smuggle in illegal gaming devices or alcohol during Prohibition. They also came in handy when stars and politicians wanted to secretly visit the lodge. And the ghosts? They are certainly there. I've investigated the Cal Neva tunnel numerous times, and there is always the heaviness associated with haunted locations. People walking through the tunnel have felt cold spots and have been brushed up against too many times to ever deny that the tunnel is haunted. The only question is the identities of the ghosts.

Frank Sinatra's Dressing Room

It's not every day that you get to visit the dressing room of a star. The first time I came into this room, I admit to being a bit—just a bit—star struck. It seems to be large for a dressing room. But then again, it belonged to Frank Sinatra, and this is where the star himself got ready for his performances. It's said that we leave imprints wherever we go. These psychic impressions can be sensed, or read, by those who are gifted in this way.

The mirror in the dressing room is surrounded by blazing, round lights and is thought to be the same mirror that Sinatra stared into. Needless to say, it has been used by many people since Sinatra called it his. So when the psychics who investigated the dressing room sensed an unfriendly presence, I doubted they were picking up his presence. Perhaps it was mobster Sam Giancana or one of his henchmen, who hangs out here as well as backstage.

Time-Warp Ghosts in the Pit

For those who aren't familiar with the term "pit" as it is used in casinos, the pit refers to a group of blackjack tables that are usually set up in a circular or semicircular arrangement. Inside the circle, behind the tables, stand the card dealers. Hovering behind the dealers are their supervisors (pit bosses), whose jobs are to watch all the action. The customers (card players) are, of course, on the outside of the circle.

The following story is an interesting, if somewhat unusual sighting:

I was walking toward the pit, and as I got closer to a certain blackjack table, I saw several people who looked like they had just stepped out of the 1940s. They were playing cards and laughing and talking, but it was funny, I couldn't hear a word they were saying.

I asked the dealer who they were, but from his reaction, it was obvious he didn't know what I was talking about. I stepped to the other side of the pit and looked back, and the people had disappeared. Every time I walked past that table, I saw the same people involved in gambling. It was weird; I think they were some sort of time-warp ghosts or something. Apparently, no one could see them but me.

They moved that table out of the pit last year, and I haven't seen the people since. If you ask me, I guess they were somehow attached to that table.

Did she see something similar to place-memory ghosts? Or were they actually haunting the blackjack table?

Swimming Marilyn

Sightings of the ghostly Marilyn Monroe were regularly reported near the Cal Neva's swimming pool. I've never seen a photograph of Monroe entering, exiting or swimming in the pool at the Cal Neva. This doesn't mean that such a photograph doesn't exist or that she didn't enjoy the pool. The sightings might mean that while she didn't swim here in life, she wanted to, and she is making up for lost time in death. According to those who saw the blond actress's apparition, she swims from one side of the pool to the other, steps up to the rail and vanishes.

A man who stayed at the Cal Neva years ago claimed to have been swimming alone in the pool one night when he looked across the water and saw Marilyn Monroe swimming toward him. "I knew who it was right away. I was stunned that I couldn't do anything but stare at her. As she swam closer, she smiled and then just like that, she was gone. It was one of the strangest things I've ever seen."

Aside from the ghostly Marilyn Monroe, this pool is also interesting because it is probably the only place in the United States where one can swim across a state line with such ease. A boundary line separating California and

Nevada is painted on the bottom of the pool. The Cal Neva remodeling plans call for the swimming pool to be filled in and a new pool will be placed at a different location on the property.

How this will affect the swimming Monroe ghost, we can only imagine.

Reality TV Back in the Day

Luck plays a big part in most everything we do in life, along with planning and preparation, of course. I got lucky in ghost hunting several years ago when I got the opportunity to thoroughly investigate the Cal Neva. I had prepared only in the fact that I was familiar with the Cal Neva's history. I hadn't really planned on the phone call I received from Indigo Films. Of course, I was thrilled when the company asked if I would be interested in taking part in a television show it was doing on the ghosts and hauntings of the Cal Neva Resort for the Travel Channel. I didn't need time to think it over; I agreed at once. This was a time when ghost investigations were still new and a curiosity. It was before television shows featuring ghost hunters became regular viewing fare.

On the day of the shoot, my husband, a friend and I drove to the Cal Neva Lodge and met with the film crew. Another friend would be playing the part of Marilyn Monroe's ghost. She had beaten us to the lodge and was already in the showroom selecting her costume. The first area to be filmed was the Indian Room, with its large fireplace and its California/Nevada state line marker than divides the room in half. Previous EVP meter readings indicated there was ghostly activity in the room. We walked around the room a few times taking pictures and trying to get a feel for it. The director briefly explained what she wanted, and the cameras were rolling.

"Come toward me fast. Now turn and walk away. Stop! Now do it again. OK turn this way. Stop!"

"Do you really think this place is haunted?" a cameraman asked.

"Yes, but maybe not this room so much." I didn't feel a thing in the Indian Room; besides, we were anxious to get to Monroe's cabin.

Time was flying. While they set up the next scene, my friend and I talked, forgetting that we were wearing microphones. Embarrassing yes, especially when one of the sound men informed us that they could hear us. "You're mic-ed!" he said with a chuckle.

A lesson learned; we weren't actors. After a few more takes, we broke for lunch. At the table, we talked ghosts and swapped stories from previous investigations. Yes, it's true—cameras, recorders and other such equipment have been known to malfunction in places that are haunted.

"Ever seen a ghost?" That's the standard question. "Uh, I'm not sure, what about you?" And that's the equally standard, noncommittal answer.

Lunch was over, and we were ready to explore Monroe's cabin. Those who've read any of my other books know that I believe we all possess a certain amount of psychic ability to one degree or other. I don't consider myself any more, or less, sensitive than the next person.

That said, I admit that I felt a great deal of energy in Monroe's cabin on this day. It wasn't necessarily Monroe. In the years since she slept here, thousands of other people have visited this cabin. That makes for a lot of energy. During a subsequent investigation of the cabin, a sensitive picked up on the energy in the cabin, too. "I don't think Marilyn is here tonight," she told us calmly. We agreed. "But she drops in from time to time," the sensitive added.

THUNDERBIRD LODGE AND GEORGE WHITTELL

During the Depression while much of the country struggled to put food on the table, George Whittell inherited roughly $30 million, more money than he could ever spend. Born to a life of privilege and wealth, Whittell had it all. From the day of his birth to that of his death, his every whim, no matter how eccentric, was indulged. A notorious playboy, George Whittell made two bad marriages before finally marrying Elyia in 1919. Their union lasted until he died in 1969.

With his father's death in 1922, forty-year-old George Whittell Jr. became a very wealthy man. Like so many other wealthy Bay Area men, Whittell wanted a summer estate at Lake Tahoe. He owned forty thousand acres and twenty-seven miles of Lake Tahoe's Eastern Shore in 1936 and planned to build a summer home using some of his inherited millions. He chose one of Nevada's top architects, Frederic DeLongchamps, to design it. The prestigious Thunderbird Lodge began to take shape.

All buildings were to blend aesthetically with their surroundings, and none should detract from the beauty of the lake. Using master craftsmen and ironworkers and local stonemasons who'd learned their trade at the Stewart Indian School in Carson City, DeLongchamps made Whittell's dream a reality.

Thunderbird Lodge from a distance. *Photo by Richard St. Clair.*

The resulting Whittell Estate (also called Thunderbird Lodge) was the most fabulous residence on the lake. Here, George Whittell Jr. (or the "Captain," as he preferred to be called) entertained showbiz notables, sports figures, scoundrels, showgirls and politicians with equal aplomb. Eventually, rumors flew around the lake about the eccentric man, his parties and other outrageous goings on at the Whittell Estate. An animal lover, the Captain was said to allow his pet lion, Bill, to roam the grounds freely. As much as he loved animals, Whittell could apparently be spiteful. One story has him so angry with a neighbor on the lake that he turned up his phonograph and played the same tune over and over and over. This annoyed the neighbor and pleased the Captain.

It seems that the Captain had an eye for the ladies. It was whispered that showgirls from nearby hotels and casinos regularly strutted their stuff in the card house at the Whittell Estate. The card house was connected to the main house by a six-hundred-foot tunnel and was said to be the site of many high-stakes card games and late-night parties. When anyone drank too much, Whittell would reportedly lock them in a little jail cell located in the tunnel. This would surely sober someone up.

The Thunderbird Lodge gate. *Photo by Terri Hall-Peltier.*

Whittell loved gadgets. Even though he had drawn up plans for extensively developing the area, he decided against building hotels, casinos and resorts. Whether that decision was made with an eye toward preservation or simply as a means of keeping people and intrusion at bay, it proved fortuitous for future generations, who can enjoy the shoreline's pristine beauty, minus the high-rise building on the South Shore.

George Whittell was a private man. During his later years, he became more and more reclusive. But one of the biggest mysteries concerning Whittell was his relationship with Mae Mollhagan, his companion and secretary. Was she his lover or simply a very well paid and trusted employee? Perhaps she was both. When Mae died in an automobile accident near Incline Village in 1954, George Whittell did an odd thing. He had her wrecked Jeep hauled back to Thunderbird Lodge so that he could see it. Rumor was that he walked to the Jeep every day and talked with the ghost of Mae. To keep things somber, he ordered loud funeral music to be played over and over in her honor.

This goes along with what the Captain supposedly did when a workman fell to his death during renovation of the pool house. He ordered the room immediately sealed up. Everything was left just as it was, with the ladder still lying at the bottom of the swimming pool. Only recently was the room unsealed. Some say the spirit of the workman haunts the pool house to this day. Admittedly, there is a strange eeriness about the room.

George Whittell Jr. died in 1969, and a private individual purchased his estate. Eventually, the estate was sold to the Thunderbird Lodge Preservation Society, a nonprofit group that oversees the lodge. Today, the Captain's fabulous estate is open to the public, and guided tours are offered from the Tuesday before Memorial Day until mid-October. Thunderbird Lodge is one tour that shouldn't be missed. Although, officially, no actual ghost sightings have been reported on the grounds of the lodge, many believe it is haunted. Items are often moved for no apparent reason and by no earthly hand.

Cold spots and feelings of being watched have been reported in the boathouse and the pool house. Two psychics have reported seeing a woman jump or fall to her death in the boathouse; others have recorded chanting, thought to be Native American in origin, there as well.

The maids' and butlers' quarters have been converted into the gift shop. Cold, unexplained drafts are sometimes felt in this building. Does Captain Whittell haunt his beloved Thunderbird Lodge? Perhaps he does and only wants to keep his fabulous home to himself. There are also those who say that Mae Mollhagan is the resident ghost here.

Investigating the Thunderbird Lodge

There was a time when I was only one of a handful of ghost investigators in the entire state of Nevada. Times change; today, there are hundreds, if not thousands, of us here in the Silver State. The following incidents took place years before the weekly television shows that feature a new location and a new ghost investigation in each episode.

I was friends with the caretaker at the Thunderbird Lodge and often there, visiting her and hunting ghosts. I believe that both George Whittell and Mae Mollhagan haunt Thunderbird. During an EVP session in the main room, the sounds of a couple bickering back and forth were recorded. This, we thought, were the voices of the Captain and Mae.

When a television show from Great Britain expressed interest in filming an episode at the lodge, we were thrilled. On the day of the shoot, I arrived and was introduced to everyone who would be involved in the filming. One of the psychics arrived late. She sashayed into the lodge and stopped in the hall. Pointing to a photograph of George Whittell, she said, "I don't like this man. He was not a very nice person."

The author, left, with Terri Hall-Peltier at the gatehouse of the Thunderbird Lodge. *Photo by Richard St. Clair.*

Our first day found us in the boathouse. It is here that numerous strange occurrences have been reported. The boathouse is eerie and cold after dark, but this was late in the day, and with bright late afternoon sunlight streaming through its windows, it takes on a less ominous aura. After we did an extensive walkthrough with the film crew, daylight was quickly slipping away. Stark shadows fell across the walls, and there was the unmistakable sound of water slapping against the boathouse. It is a rhythmic sound, and some have reported hearing drumming and chanting and cries for help emanating from it.

Later that night, we were still filming in the boathouse when an unseen force attacked the psychic who did not like George Whittell. As she screamed and ran and flailed her arms, I couldn't help but wonder if George Whittell or Mae Mollhagan was giving her a bad time for what she had said earlier.

As the night wore on, we moved into the tunnel. The lake was choppy as a storm moved across the Sierras. We were bundled up in heavy jackets as we trudged through the chilly tunnel. Someone yelled, "Stop!"

There was a feeling that someone or something malevolent was racing toward us. We stopped and listened. Two people instinctively started to run.

I held back a smile, wondering just how they intended to outrun a spirit. If a ghost was truly with us, it could move through the granite walls faster than George Whittell's sleek racing boat, *Thunderbird*, once sliced through the waters of Lake Tahoe.

Muffled voices seemed to be echoing all around us. There was an audible sigh of relief when we realized these voices were not paranormal at all but only the voices of others in the card room.

"There is something here," a psychic said.

We were just coming on the little dungeon area when the psychic smiled broadly and informed us that it was Whittell's pet lion. "He is licking my face," she said calmly.

Television crews loved the Thunderbird Lodge. It was picturesque; once owned by a reclusive, eccentric millionaire; had a great backstory; and was haunted. During another shoot at the Thunderbird, a psychic felt that a bear had killed a man on the property. It sounded like a bit of melodrama dreamed up to increase viewership, but it had happened.

On a rainy afternoon, I was at the Thunderbird Lodge with a friend. We went upstairs and split up. While I went to photograph in Whittell's bedroom, she went across the landing to his wife's (Elyia) room. She was gone only a few minutes before she came running back. "There's a crying woman in there!" she said.

"Who is it?" I asked.

"I don't know. She totally ignored me when I asked if I could help her."

"Is she a—ghost?" I asked, knowing there were only three of us in the building.

My friend nodded, "Oh, yes."

We ran back to the bedroom, but whoever she was, the crying woman had left.

Later, when we looked at the photographs of Elyia, my friend was adamant that this was not the woman she had seen. "Maybe it was Mae," she whispered.

At that time, there were no photographs of her at Thunderbird. However, we were told that she was an attractive blonde. It was a good time to break out the voice recorders, and so we did.

We posed questions: "Mae, if that was you could you tell us why you were crying? Are you sad because you miss George? Were you deliberately driving your car in the wrong lane?"

If Mae was present, she was as reticent with us as she had been earlier in Elyia's bedroom. We can only imagine why she might have been crying.

Doggie Treats

Did I mention that the Thunderbird Lodge caretaker had a large dog? During several ghost investigations, this dog proved to be as accurate as the dowsing rods. Dogs make great ghost hunters. They are sensitive to things going on around them and can often point out the best spot to use dowsing rods or record EVP. But much as we love them, dogs will be dogs.

During a long night of filming at the Thunderbird Lodge, the crew laid out a repast of cold cuts, cheeses, chips, breads, strawberries, nuts and assorted cookies so that we might eat while on break. Spread invitingly on a long table, the food would be ready when we were.

Unbeknownst to us, while we filmed in the boathouse, the caretaker's dog discovered the food. Being a rather large dog, he sauntered up to the table and helped himself. Cut! The announcement that there was food waiting had us moving quickly through the tunnel and toward that table. But, like the best laid plans of mice and men, the repast had gone awry. The caring canine had left some food, but no one had much of an appetite after that.

SUGAR PINE POINT'S GHOST

I like book signings because not only do I get to meet some of my readers but also many of them share their stories and hauntings with me. I happened to be doing a book signing at one of the local museums when an elderly man stopped by the table. He nodded, picked up a book and flipped through its pages. Carefully putting it down, he asked, "Why don't you have anything about the little girl's ghost at Sugar Pine Point?"

I'd never heard of the ghostly little girl and told him so. Technically, Sugar Pine Point is on the California side of the lake, but I was curious nonetheless. And since you never know when such information will come in handy, I urged him on.

"Please tell me about her."

"All I know is what I've been told."

I nodded encouragingly, and he continued:

> *Guess she's about eleven or twelve. She and her family were houseguests of the Hellmans. They were all sunbathing on the beach one afternoon when she and a couple of other children slipped away to swim. That was the*

A view of Lake Tahoe near Incline Village. *Photo by Bill Oberding.*

last anyone ever saw of her. The other children raised the alarm when they returned to shore without her. They searched for her over a week, but the little girl's body was never recovered. I haven't seen her, but I know some folks who have. They say she has long, straight blond hair and wears a pale

65

blue dress with a big white collar. She usually appears just before sundown, and always looks so sad.

Wealthy San Francisco businessman I.W. Hellman built his summer home, Pine Lodge, on Sugar Pine Point in 1903. On his death, he left the home to his youngest daughter, who later married Sidney Erhman. Today, the home, now known as the Erhman Mansion, is a museum in Sugar Pine Point State Park. It is located ten miles south of Tahoe City on Highway 89. Some who have worked there say the place is definitely haunted but that it is Hellman himself who haunts it.

THE GHOST OF CAPTAIN BARTER

Lake Tahoe has always attracted colorful characters. Unique among those who have lived, and died, in the Lake Tahoe area is the legendary Captain Richard Barter. Known as the "Hermit of Emerald Bay," the old sailor worked as caretaker for the Holladay family estate at Emerald Bay. When not out on the lake in his boat, *Nancy*, Barter enjoyed whiskey and tall tales. The more he drank, the wilder his tales became. One such story involved the loss of his toes.

In his years spent on Emerald Bay, the old man had several brushes with death while out on the water. When his toes became severely frozen during an accident that nearly killed him, Captain Barter realized amputation was necessary and calmly cut them off with a butcher knife. Thereafter, he kept them as souvenirs and showed them to shocked visitors as evidence of his miraculous survival. "Them's my toes," he proudly proclaimed.

Whenever he faced danger on the lake, luck had always been on his side. But as any gambler knows, good luck doesn't last forever. It can turn bad in an instant. Captain Barter's luck ran out one stormy night in October 1873. He had spent the evening drinking with friends at a bar across the lake. Others might be intimidated by foul weather, but he wasn't. He had made the trip across Emerald Bay countless times before and didn't give the weather a second thought as he climbed into his boat and began rowing toward home. He was almost there when a sudden swell came up and capsized the *Nancy*. An expert swimmer who knew the lake better than just about anyone, Captain Barter wasn't worried. Even on wintry days, when others were afraid to do so, he would jump in the cold water and swim.

Emerald Bay, Lake Tahoe. *Photo by Michael Marfell.*

This time it was different. The storm was severe. While he desperately tried to swim to safety, his little boat was battered to pieces on the rocks at Rubicon Point. He fought for his life, but he was no match for the angry, icy waters that churned around him. Exhausted, his body paralyzed by the cold, the old sailor perished in the 1,400-foot depths of the mountain lake he had loved.

Like those of so many other Lake Tahoe drowning victims before (and since) him, Captain Barter's body was never recovered. In a particularly cruel twist of fate, the man who had designed his own crypt and memorial burial spot years before would never rest there. Years later, his crypt was destroyed so that the wealthy Lora Knight's teahouse could be built on the island across from her Vikingsholm estate.

It's said that on foggy mornings and evenings, Captain Barter's ghost rises from the depths of Lake Tahoe and wanders its shores in search of that burial site he built for himself so long ago.

Escorting Elvis

My friend Cimarron Sam—who is part of Empathic Paranormal, one of northern Nevada's most respected paranormal teams—is also a very gifted medium who shared the following stories with me:

It's the Hard Rock Hotel now, but when I was hired as security, it was the Horizon; before that, it was the Sahara. Part of my job was to check out disturbances. My dispatcher was a three-hundred-pound woman who took no guff from anyone. She was one tough cookie. One night, she called me to the booth and said, "I have to send you down to the pit—but I have to warn you, I don't like going down there."

"Why?" I asked

"There's something down there I don't want to deal with."

The pit was down stairs where a stage came out of the ground. At one time, performers would walk onto the stage, and it would be raised up to the showroom where the audiences awaited. Around this area was a twenty-foot cement floor you could fall through if you weren't careful. So when someone heard kids running around down there, we had to check it out.

I walked down the staircase and came in[to] the hallway. Immediately, the hair on my neck stood up. I walked by the old dressing rooms. I looked around but didn't see any kids. I walked on. When I got about twenty feet away from the stage, it sounded like I was dragging something, so I stopped to see if I had anything stuck to my shoe. At this moment, I was in a heightened sense of awareness. I kept walking, and I kept hearing the same sound. What is that, I wondered. Telling myself to get out, I picked up my pace; the sound increased. I started to sprint. The dragging sound was coming faster until it was upon me. I stopped and looked around. There was nothing.

I flew up the stairs and raced back to the booth.

"Did you find those kids?" the dispatcher asked.

"No," I said. "But there was something down there. It sounded like I was dragging something. It sounded almost like plastic."

She smiled, "Do you know this was the old Sahara?"

I shook my head.

"Elvis used to perform here."

Oh my God, I thought. It was Elvis's cape dragging along. Yes, that was it. It was like I was wearing a cape and it was dragging along.

"You see," she smiled. "Elvis thought you were his escort to the stage. When you stopped, he stopped. When you ran, he ran. You're not the only one to have encountered him. The maintenance men—everyone has experienced this. You were escorting Elvis."

Elvis performed at the Horizon many times. His apparition has appeared to employees throughout the hotel. He was reportedly seen and heard so often on the seventh floor that no one thought much about the King's ghost. Now that the Horizon has been transformed into the Hard Rock, we will see if Elvis continues his stay.

Ghost in the Room on the Third Floor

Cimarron Sam also told of an incident in one of the Horizon's hotel rooms:

One night I got called up to a room on the third floor. A woman was screaming so loudly that people were concerned for her safety. I went up there, and no one was there. The room was empty. No one was booked into this particular room that night. Later, I found out that a hotel maid who had broken up with her boyfriend had been hiding from him in this room. The break up was nasty. While she was waiting to get a restraining order, she had checked into the hotel. But he found her and came up and killed her in the room—the maids didn't like to even come into the room because they would hear her crying and screaming.

A lot of things like that went on at the Horizon. A man from New York found out his wife was cheating on him, so he drained their life savings, came and gambled it all away, then committed suicide in a room on the fifth or sixth floor.

Incidentally, another friend who works in the hospitality industry at South Lake Tahoe told me that when the Horizon was being converted into the Hard Rock Hotel recently, carpenters, electricians and others were continually telling her about the ghostly occurrences that were taking place in the building, especially in the small tower in the back. This isn't surprising; ghost researchers know that one way to stir up ghostly activity is to remodel. But this would lead me to believe that Elvis isn't the only specter at the hotel.

NICK OF THE WOODS

They say that necessity is the mother of invention. This may be particularly true in matters of marketing strategy. When Ephraim "Yank" Clement purchased Martin Smith's way station in 1859, he hoped his new establishment, Yank's Station, would prosper. The sharp-eyed Clement noticed that tourists were converging on the area to gawk at Shakespeare Rock, and he wanted a similar draw. Over centuries, nature had conveniently carved out a profile on the majestic rock that was said to resemble the bard himself.

If the hand of nature could create a masterpiece once, it could surely repeat the process. Clement walked his property searching for something that would lead more tourists and money in his direction.

Yank's Station in the valley of Lake Tahoe, El Dorado County, 1866. *Photo by Lawrence and Houseworth. Library of Congress.*

The way station sat in a picturesque green meadow near the shore, and apparently, that was all there was going to be. But then Clement spotted a strange tree that would come to be known as "Nick of the Woods."

Word soon got out, and tourists began coming to Yank's Station for a look at the unusual tree. Of Nick, Dan De Quille had the following to say in his *The Big Bonanza*:

> *At "Yank's Station" on the Placerville road, a short distance from the shore of the lake, is to be seen a most singular freak of nature to which the name "Nick of the Woods" has been given. It is a large knot in a crotch of cedar tree, which forks a few feet from the ground, but it looks like a work of art. It startlingly resembles the head of an old man. In looking upon this marvel of nature we can very easily imagine it to be some hoary-headed old sinner thus wedged into the crotch of the tree and imprisoned for all time on account of some grievous offense committed about the time that he was thus placed in the stocks. So natural and perfect is this head of an old man, and such an expression of patient suffering is seen in every feature of the face, that many persons will not believe that it is wholly the work of nature until after having closely examined it.*

The old way station is long gone, and Nick of the Woods is no more. Today, a golf course covers most of the area where the tree once grew.

WATCHER OF THE WOODS

Love and respect for nature are part of Native American culture. My friend Cimarron Sam, of Empathic Paranormal, who happens to be Native American, shared this story of a tree with me:

> *The tree is a Sequoia tree. It's in an area of forest behind Sierra Tract* [one of the area's oldest neighborhoods] *in South Lake Tahoe. It is just before Trout Creek and to the left of Trout Creek Meadow. We had heard about the tree—the Watcher of the Woods—so we went to see it. When you walk to it, you sense it is a mystical place. It's very quiet and has its own atmosphere.*
>
> *It is one of the original trees in the area, and it resonates its own energy. People bring quartz crystals to recharge them. You'll find dead carcasses*

The Watcher of the Woods mystical tree. *Photo by Richard St. Clair.*

around the tree because people bring the carcasses and other things to energize the tree. The tree is dying, and they are bringing these offerings trying to keep it alive.

My friend warned me never to take any of these offerings. Bad luck would happen if I did.

After Cimarron shared this story, my friend Terri Hall-Peltier and I decided we had to see it. On a recent warm late-spring day, our friend Richard St. Clair (also of Empathic Paranormal) drove us to the tree. Sadly, once we located it, the tree looked as if it were dead. It was an evergreen, yet the branches were bare. There is a stillness surrounding this tree. We brought no offerings, just our respect. As we photographed the tall sequoia, we realized that the tree's days were most likely numbered. It will probably have to be taken down. It's sad to think that this tree has been here since John Frémont discovered Lake Tahoe, since Abraham Lincoln fought for Nevada to become a state, since man walked on the moon—and now, it's dead. The cause is probably the severe drought the area has been experiencing. We walked back to the Jeep, hoping we were wrong about the tree, yet knowing that we were right.

One thing I have to add here: my Sony camera was only half charged when I started out on this day. After taking several photos, I worried the camera would fade on me at a most inopportune moment. It didn't. When I got back home that evening, I discovered my camera was fully charged. How could this be? I have no explanation—only that it happened.

GHOST ON THE SIDE OF THE ROAD

The strange story of a young woman's ghost who saved her young son's life has been featured on several television shows over the years, including *Unsolved Mysteries*.

On a summer night in 1994, a woman was driving along the mountainous Highway 50 in the El Dorado National Forest. As her car approached Bullion Bend, she noticed something odd: a glowing, naked woman was lying on the side of the road. Wondering why on earth someone would be out without a stitch of clothing on, she drove on until she could stop and notify the sheriff's department. But when officers arrived at the location, they found no naked woman—nothing.

The next morning, they returned to the old stage road known as Bullion Bend to renew their search. This time, they discovered only a child's shoe. Meanwhile, Christine Skubish and her three-year-old son were still missing. It had been several days since the young woman left Placerville with her son and headed up through Tahoe. Their family was growing concerned. As the search intensified, the sheriffs noticed that there were no skid marks indicating a wreck had occurred.

Then someone walked to the edge of the cliff and looked down. There, at the bottom of a forty-foot drop, the wreckage was spotted.

Christine Skubish was dead behind the wheel. Apparently, she had fallen asleep and driven off the road. In the backseat was her three-year-old son, very much alive, thirsty and hungry.

There are many theories as to what happened that June night on Bullion Bend. Did the ghost of Christine Skubish appear on the roadside in order to get help for her young son? Or was it the child's guardian angel, perhaps? Another possibility is that the passing motorist only imagined a woman lying on the side of the road; this would be a mind-boggling coincidence. As a mother and a ghost investigator, I'm opting for the ghost theory; it seems the most logical.

CRASH

Almost one hundred years after the Donner Party tragedy, the worst aviation disaster in the Lake Tahoe area's history happened on a snowy first day of March 1964. "Only three hundred feet higher"—that's what experts said about the ill-fated airliner that crashed into Genoa Peak (three miles east of Kingsbury Grade), killing everyone on board.

Earlier that morning, Flight 901A Paradise Airlines Constellation N86504 took off from Oakland en route to Tahoe Valley Airport, 149 miles away. There were no empty seats. On board were four crewmen and eighty-one passengers who were headed for a fun weekend of gambling and skiing.

A late-winter storm swept across the California coast, and heavy snow was falling in the Sierras. Visibility was limited. As high winds raged across the region, the tower informed the crew that there was zero visibility at the airport. The pilot replied that he was "holding over Tahoe."

And then, he made a fateful decision. He either attempted to land at the Tahoe Valley Airport or divert to Reno until the weather cleared. His last transmission was brief, "Flight 901…"

The radio tower lost communication as the aircraft slammed into Genoa Peak. According to experts, the plane could easily have cleared the mountain ridge had it been flying only three hundred feet higher. There was no voice recorder on board, but later, as investigators combed through the wreckage, they discovered a problem with the plane's altimeter.

One Genoa resident remembers the day well. "I was going to get the sheep when I heard a loud bang. I didn't know it was a plane crash until I heard the news the next day."

The day after the crash, search-and-rescue teams located the snow-covered wreckage. They had held out hope but immediately realized that this was not to be a rescue mission but one of recovery. The work of locating the bodies and bringing them down the mountain began. It would be three weeks before all were recovered and identified.

The area of the crash is desolate. Those who've been up there tell of an eerie quiet, even to this day. Ghosts of flight 901A are said to haunt the community center in Minden.

AL TAHOE CEMETERY

Think about the movie *Poltergeist*. Ghostly activity happened because houses were built atop a cemetery. Moving from the realm of fiction, let's look at the Black Hope Cemetery haunting in Texas. When a subdivision was created and built on an African American cemetery, weird things started to happen once the homes were occupied. There were strange noises, threatening apparitions and foul smells. It's not always wise to build on a cemetery.

But it seems to have worked out OK with the old Al Tahoe Cemetery. While the cemetery has been downsized to make room for the living, a sewer line was dug through it, and Alameda Street runs through a corner of the cemetery, residents don't experience ghostly activity here—certainly nothing like what happened in *Black Hope* or *Poltergeist*. This isn't to say that there is no activity; there is. Over the years, residents have reported noises and thumps that defy explanation (maybe to them, but not to us). It's worth a stop to take a peek at the tiny cemetery and see how progress treats the dead.

SIERRA HOUSE SPIRITS

In the winter of 1858, Robert Garwood Dean of Genoa came looking for a spot to build a way station. He decided on a spot on the old Emigrant Ridge Route and the Daggett Ravine Trail. He had chosen wisely; his way station sat in a pine-covered meadow near Cold Creek, just a few miles from Lake Tahoe. When the Sierra House way station was completed in the summer of 1859, it was destined to become one of the most famous stations on this particular route from Nevada to California. But Robert Garwood Dean would not be part of it. He sold the way station after only a year of ownership. Legendary stagecoach driver Hank Monk made regular stops at the Sierra House, as did some of the area's most despicable bad men. Sam Brown and James Stewart, better known as the "Silent Terror," were two killers who found the accommodations at Sierra House to their liking.

Over the years, the way station was remodeled and added on to by several different owners. Many people stopped in at the Sierra House. A few of them have decided to stay on. A caretaker who lived on the premises in the early 1900s insisted that he'd seen spectral visitors walk in and out of the old building. According to the frightened man, these spirits rattled windows and banged on the doors. The Sierra House is gone; its last remnants were destroyed more than fifty years ago.

What became of the old way station's spectral visitors is anyone's guess. And so I will—guess, that is. I've heard many people say, "I don't understand why my house is haunted. I live in a new house. How can it be haunted?"

A home may be brand new, but the land on which it stands is not. Ghosts that once made themselves at home in a building that no longer stands may decide to haunt the new one that is erected. Today, homes and other buildings cover much of the land that James Garwood Dean first came upon during that long-ago winter. Perhaps some of these places are home to the Sierra House spirits.

HAUNTED MOTEL

Standing in the shadows of large hotel casinos is a motel that offers no-frills rooms and cut-rate prices. It's not the fanciest, but it's clean and a great find for the budget conscious. Like so many of the larger hotels in this area, it is haunted. Unbeknownst to the management, a dying woman checked in one night and was dead the next morning. When she failed to appear at the allotted eleven o'clock checkout time, the manager waited a few more hours before knocking on her door. Receiving no answer, he unlocked the door and found her in her room "dead and bleeding from every orifice."

A month passed. A tourist who was passing through on her way back east was given the room. The next morning, she came down to the office to say, "I don't know if you know it or not, but my room is haunted. I woke up to see this woman staring down at me." When offered another room, she declined. "I don't mind ghosts as long as they leave me alone."

While some guests are oblivious to her, others have complained about the ghost in this particular room, saying that she hovers over the bed, staring intently.

Although those in the hospitality industry are generally reluctant to talk about it, people die in motels and hotels more often than you might think. This woman was not the first person to die in a motel or hotel, and she certainly won't be the last. This is one reason motels and hotels are so haunted.

3
TRUCKEE

TIMBER

Truckee, California, is a small town with a big history. It was named in honor of Paiute chief Truckee, who helped hundreds of emigrants safely cross into California. Chief Truckee also acted as a guide for explorer Captain Frémont. For the unfamiliar, Truckee is pronounced so that it rhymes with the word "lucky." Truckee offers visitors historic hotels, motels, quaint bed-and-breakfasts, restaurants and bars. Shops housed in century-old buildings line Commercial Street. All of them offer countless items for the big-city tourists who flock here during the two seasons: summer shopping and winter skiing.

If not for the rich forests in the Lake Tahoe/Truckee area, mining in Virginia City would not have succeeded. In 1860, Virginia City's mining operations were faced with the problem of safely removing precious ore from deep within the earth. No sooner had a miner begun to use his pickaxe than the soft dirt in the mine fell down on him. All previous methods of mining the rich ore were useless. Without a clever idea, Comstock mining would be doomed. With the prospect of financial loss looming overhead, a manager of the Ophir Mining Company asked Philip Deidesheimer, a German engineer, to come to Virginia City and devise a system for successfully mining the ore.

When Deidesheimer arrived, he was put in charge as mining superintendent and immediately went to work solving the problem at hand.

Within a few weeks, he'd come up with a relatively simple solution to the mining company's dilemma. His square-set timbering method involved interlocking frame boxes that could be stacked in any direction—one on top of the other or side by side—like a honeycomb. Deidesheimer's invention made one thing very clear: timber, and lots of it, would be needed.

There wasn't an abundance of trees in the Comstock area, but the forests on the western slope of the Sierras near Lake Tahoe were thick with tall pines. Astute businessmen were quick to realize how valuable the timber was not only to the burgeoning railroad but also to Virginia City's mining operations. Lumber companies were formed, sawmills were built and hundreds of lumberjacks were hired for the purpose of providing the much-needed timber. Thousands of acres of pine forest were cleared. Soon the lumber companies, too, were faced with a dilemma: finding a better, more cost-effective method for delivering the timber to the Comstock.

That method came in 1867 when J.W. Haines constructed his ingenious V flume. Now, lumber could be quickly transported from the Tahoe region to Carson City and Reno, where it would be loaded onto railcars and hauled up to the Comstock.

Haines patented his V flume on September 20, 1870. Two years later, in August 1872, he brought a lawsuit in the United States District Court against William Sharon and others he felt had infringed on his patented invention. As the inventor, Haines believed that he had the right of certain benefits. The flume, he argued, had enabled logging companies to transport wood more cost effectively. The Yerrington Company had moved over thirty thousand cords of wood in two years at a cost of less than one dollar per cord. This was a fraction of what the old cost of transporting lumber had been.

W.N. Leete's testimony described the V flume as "constructed of planks nailed together in the shape of the letter V, with the ends of the section butted together, so as to form a smooth channel."

Testimony indicated that V flumes in Musgrove Canyon and Washoe County predated Haines's by at least four years. Their builders may not have realized the improvement of the V flume over the box flume, but the fact that they had been using them prior to Haines's V flume led Judge Field to rule Haines's patent invalid and to find for the defendants.

Like Philipp Deidesheimer, Haines would never become rich from his ingenious idea. He was not doomed to failure though. J.W. Haines later served as a Douglas County state senator. With the introduction of the V flume, Tahoe's remote forests and canyons became accessible to the lumber companies. The clearing of these areas continued. In 1875, the Pacific Wood and Lumber Company built one of the largest flumes in the area. The flume cost $250,000 and covered a length of fifteen miles. It carried over 500,000 feet of lumber each day; two thousand horses would have been needed to do this same amount of work.

Truckee was an early railroad lumber town that grew and developed within a few miles of the 1846 Donner Party encampment site. With the rich ore discovery in Gold Canyon (near Virginia City), mining began in earnest on the Comstock. This increased demand for lumber meant an economic boom for Truckee. The town had a rowdy reputation, but jobs were plentiful as lumber mills kept busy supplying the Comstock and Sacramento areas.

There was a downside to the boom. Criminals also came to the area, seeking riches and opportunity. Shootings and robberies were commonplace along Truckee's red-light district on Jibboom Street. Alarmed citizens were not about to tolerate such behavior. The 601 Vigilance Committee was formed to stem the tide of rampant lawlessness. Like its Virginia City counterpart, the 601 left warnings for those who were not wanted in town.

Filmmakers invariably chose the Truckee area when looking for locations that resembled the Yukon. In 1923, a film crew came to Truckee to shoot the silent film *Call of the Wild*, based on Jack London's highly acclaimed novel. A year later, Charlie Chaplin's classic silent film *The Gold Rush* was filmed, in part, around Truckee during the late winter and early spring of 1924. The idea for the movie is said to have come to Chaplin while reading a book on the plight of the Donner Party. During his stay, the comedian and his crew were said to have visited many bars and restaurants in town. Some say that the comedian slept in his private railcar; others insist that he stayed in Truckee's hotels. He is only one of many filmmakers who have been captivated by the Truckee area's picturesque beauty.

THE GHOSTS OF CHARLES CHARLTON AND WILLIAM SMITH

In 1877, William Smith and his wife shared a house on High Street in Truckee with Charles Charlton and his wife. While their wives got along well with each other, the two men did not. They argued all the time. One September night, they got into an argument that escalated into violence when Charles Charlton lost his temper and turned his pistol on William Smith, killing him. He was remorseful afterward, but it was too late for the deceased Smith. There was nothing left to do but turn himself in to Justice Keiser, who promptly had Charlton transported to the county jail in Nevada City.

There, he was to stand trial for murder, but Charlton had other plans. As the days and nights wore on, guilt got the better of him. The only thing he could do was end it all, so he did. Charlton hanged himself in his cell. But this was not the end of the Charlton/Smith saga.

The widows of Smith and Charlton continued to live in the house on High Street—that is, they lived there until the ghostly Smith began making nightly rounds. The October 3, 1877 issue of the *Truckee Republican* carried the following story:

"Haunted"

The wives of Smith and Charlton, who have occupied the same premise wherein Charlton killed Smith a few days ago, claim that the ghostly figure of Smith frequently visits the house making most hideous noises and causing them the greatest consternation. Some people who seem to have a desire to worry the women, have sent them occasional purported telegrams from Nevada City in which is set forth the fact of Charlton's suicide by hanging which coming to them during their nervous excitement has caused their horror to know no bounds. It is said they cannot be persuaded to go near the building at present but have taken quarters elsewhere and are still in momentary fear of seeing the vision of Smith where they are now.

WALKING WITH A GHOST OR...?

Ghost hunters know better than to expect every house will be haunted. Not everything that frightens us and goes bump in the night is a ghost. Sometimes, there really is a logical explanation for what we perceive as a ghost—sometimes.

He had visited every saloon in town and had had too much to drink. It was time for him to head back home, so the young man started walking toward his room on River Street. It was late May, and the weather was finally warming up. But this was eleven o'clock at night; any warmth had long since dissipated. Even in his alcohol-induced euphoria, he shivered. And then he saw it—a glowing white figure moving toward him. As the thing got closer, he could see that it was wearing a long white robe. As the May 26, 1877 issue of the *Truckee Republican* reported:

> *His eyes bugged out, his knees became rickety and his knotted and combined locks became as stiff as fence rail. He tried to yell but he couldn't. Having stood in this unpleasant situation for several minutes watching the silent phantom, he observed another figure emerge from and adjoining house and approach the specter. A sudden start, and then some words and then both went back into the house. It turned out to be a sleepwalker.*

OLD TRUCKEE JAIL

I've never quite figured out why so many jails and prisons are haunted. It could be that the ghosts are hoping for a do-over or are afraid to move on. Whatever the reasons, places like Alcatraz, Eastern State Penitentiary and the Ohio State Penitentiary house some ghostly inmates. To this mix, I'll add the old Truckee Jail. Built in 1875, the jail served as Truckee's detention center until 1964. Used for continuously for eighty-nine years, it was in use longer than any other jail in the state of California. In that time, some very bad hombres cooled their heels here within the jail's thirty-two-inch-thick walls. Just to be on the safe side, the walls are steel lined. There is no escaping here.

The most famous guests are probably Baby Face Nelson and Machine Gun Kelly. Kelly purportedly got caught shoplifting and ended up spending a night in the local hoosegow. Nelson's infraction was minor as well. It wasn't until he'd been released that the jailers realized who he was and that he had used an alias.

A few inmates have called it quits in the old jail. One of the strangest ways to bid adieu to this world was the suicide chosen by one E.W. Duke Thompson, who died of holding his breath. Could he be one of the ghosts that hang out at the old jail today? Then again, the ghostly activity could be related to none other than Juanita Spinelli, aka Duchess, who, along with her gang of cutthroats, was apprehended by the highway patrol in Truckee and escorted to the jail. In an article in the *Sierra Sun* from November 26, 1998, entitled "Belated Tales of Truckee's Old Jail: From Gangsters to Runaway Kids," Leo Poppoff tells of Spinelli's capture on an April night in 1940 when Spinelli and her family found themselves stranded in a broken-down car on the highway.

The Truckee Old Jail Museum in Truckee, California. *Photo by Bill Oberding.*

A side view of the old Truckee jail. *Photo by Bill Oberding.*

A highway patrolman happened along and took pity on them. But bad luck—the hotels in Truckee were full. Barrett quickly found them a room at a Reno motel. Then the patrolman took them to the motel in Reno. Upon his return to Truckee, he discovered that the family was that of Ma Spinelli and her notorious gang of thieves and murderers. And they were wanted. Barrett drove back to Reno and tricked Ma and the gang into returning to Truckee with him. And that's how Spinelli and her gang came to spend some time in the old Truckee Jail.

In 1941, the murderous Spinelli finally paid for her life of crime when she became the first woman to see the inside of the California's gas chamber at San Quentin. The cold-hearted killer did not live to tell of her experience within the chamber. However, Warden Clinton Duffy did talk. Of Spinelli, he said, "She was the coldest, hardest character, male or female, that I have ever known and was utterly lacking in feminine appeal."

Psychics who've visited the old jail have felt the strong presence of a sad spirit so filled with regret that it is unable to move on. This spirit is probably not responsible for the following incident. According to one rumor, women who are especially pretty will sometimes find themselves being groped by ghostly hands in the old jail. Hmm. Some of you may be wondering how you slap a ghost's face. Good question, but I have no answer.

TRUCKEE HOTEL

The Truckee Hotel was built in 1873. In those years, it has had several owners and just as many names: the American House, the New Whitney, Hotel Blume, the Riverside Hotel and the Alpine Riverside. In 1909, when most of the hotel was destroyed by fire, the hotel went up in flames. Within forty-two days, it was rebuilt and reopened.

Featuring thirty-seven guest rooms on four floors, the hotel is an elegant reminder of how life was back in the day. Moody's Bistro is a restaurant located in the hotel. Named after John F. Moody, the original builder of the Truckee Hotel, Moody's offers a nice mix of entrées and live music and events.

In 2004, former Beatle Paul McCartney was in the Tahoe area for a ski vacation with his wife. Imagine how thrilled diners at Moody's were when Sir Paul stepped up to the mic with the band for an impromptu concert. He sang a song called "Truckee Blues" and had fun with it. Like fellow

The Truckee Hotel. *Photo by Bill Oberding.*

Englishman Charlie Chaplin decades before him, McCartney was the toast of Truckee that night. The story was picked up by news media across the country and was featured in *People Magazine.*

As for those hauntings—as wild as Truckee's past was, the most popular resident ghost at the Truckee Hotel is not that of a jealous lover, a gangster or a prostitute. The ghost is that of a little girl who drowned in the bathtub of room 403. There is some debate as to whether the child's death was an accident or murder. EVP that has been captured in the hotel doesn't offer any clue. Other paranormal activity includes flickering lights and ghostly guests that play football. Some of those who've stayed at the hotel say that certain rooms are colder than might be expected. It's not unexpected to ghost hunters who realize this is a telltale sign of a haunting.

A HAUNTED HOUSE

Haunted houses are newsworthy, especially at Halloween. Here's one haunting that took place on a long ago night somewhere in Truckee. On April 10, 1873, the *Truckee Republican* carried the following story:

Several days ago we alluded to a haunted house in Truckee and spiritual manifestations going on therein. Since then, in the same house, there have been some extraordinary and startling developments. The voices of children at times crying as if for bread, and for fear of being abducted and torn from their parents have been heard beneath the floor of the house. Recently one of the occupants of a bedroom in the house was startled from his slumbers in the middle of the night by the entrance of a man, of a gigantic size carrying a tin lantern, which cast a glaring light over the entire room. The occupant of the room, a strong, stalwart man and known among his friends to be courageous, was paralyzed with fear and unable to move. After the giant had gazed at him for a minute, the occupant of the bed recovered his courage and self-possession and seizing a heavy can by his bedside sprang up and dealt a tremendous blow at the unwelcome intruder.

The supposed ghost, spirit, demon, devil or whatever it was, showed fight and throwing his bare and icy arms around the man flung him to the floor and held him there as if in a vice. The pinioned man, in horror, shouted or rather screamed for help, and managed to reach his pistol which lay in a chair near his bed. He cocked the weapon, pulled the trigger and fired. At that moment a friend who slept in an adjoining house, having heard an unusual noise, made his appearance at the door and burst it open. The ghost had disappeared, but his victim still remained on the floor, panting, exhausted and horror-stricken. Tangible evidence of a severe struggle was visible in the room—chairs were overturned, the bedding torn from the bed, and light revealed spurts of blood upon the floor. It was over an hour before the man, who had been thus seriously handled, revived sufficiently to relate his fearful encounter. We are not permitted to give his name in this issue, nor the locality of the houses where this strange phenomenon took place, but have permission to do so if any further ghostly manifestations should occur.

Another incident that took place about the same time involved a family that was living in this house on the hill. The family members reported that they had experienced "manifestations of a mysterious and unaccountable nature." All the doors and windows were locked. No one had entered or exited the house; the family was alone. Yet they were constantly bombarded by the sounds of children weeping and of furniture being tossed about. These occurrences wreaked havoc on the family's peace of mind. Eventually, they decided to move on. We have no way of knowing the exact locations where these incidents took place. It is all but impossible to investigate these cases any further. But if someone in Truckee should ever encounter a place with disembodied voices and an angry ghost spoiling for a fight, the locations will have been found.

RICHARDSON HOUSE

Perched on a hill overlooking the town, the Richardson House was built by Warren Richardson in 1887, making it one of Truckee's oldest buildings. In 1851, Richardson and his brother, George, came west in search of gold. When their quest met with failure, they settled in Truckee, where they discovered the importance of timber to the Comstock mining companies. They started a box factory as well as the largest lumber mill in Truckee. Through their hard work, the Richardson brothers became two of the area's wealthiest men.

Ghost enthusiasts and history buffs enjoy the ambiance of the Richardson House. The quaint vacation home is rumored to be the residence of at least two ghosts. Both specters are friendly and unobtrusive. Some say that Maggie, the first wife of Warren Richardson, haunts the house in hopes of finding her child who died there so long ago. But the ghost most often encountered by visitors is that of an elderly woman who happened to be a dear friend of past owners. During one of her visits, she fell ill. Thinking it was nothing more serious than exhaustion from traveling for so long, she bid her hosts goodnight and went to bed early. The next morning, their normally punctual friend didn't come down to breakfast. Snow that had fallen throughout the night lay in deep drifts. It was an ideal day for staying in bed later than usual, so her friends decided to let her sleep. When the clock chimed 10:00 a.m., with still no sign of their guest, they became alarmed and went upstairs to wake her. There, they found her lying cold and dead in the big four-poster bed. Apparently, she'd died shortly after turning in for the night. Now, it seems that she's decided to be a permanent houseguest. While the ghostly woman usually shows up in one particular room, she has been known to roam the building.

She is probably not responsible for the moving brass urn. Twice, former owners have returned home to find the old brass urn moved from its spot on a shelf to the middle of the dining room table. Most likely, this is the work of two ghostly children who are said to have died in the house.

Several years ago, I interviewed an owner of the Richardson House who said:

It was Christmastime, and we were staying in the Writer's Room. Late that night, my husband woke me to tell me that he thought someone was in the building. He said it sound like something was being broken downstairs. I didn't hear anything, so I just rolled over and went back to sleep. Next morning, we discovered that our Christmas tree had been tipped over and every one of the glass balls had been broken.

GHOSTS IN THE GATEWAY AREA

On a recent long plane ride, a friend told me about her friend who had moved into a new house in the Gateway area of Truckee. Like most new homeowners, he was happy and proud as could be—that is, he was happy until the ghost of an old woman began appearing in the kitchen. While the ghost didn't frighten him, he had to ask, "What are you doing in my kitchen?"

He received no reply. This leads me to believe that the ghost was nothing more than place memory as she went about the business of cooking and cleaning, completely unaware that she was a nuisance to the new resident. Perhaps she had lived in the location at one time or was attached to it in some other way.

There is another small house in the Gateway area that's rumored to be haunted. When a despondent husband learned that his wife was being unfaithful to him, he turned his gun not on her but on himself. This might be a decision he regrets. Some who have lived in this house say the man has never vacated the premises. His specter has been seen walking through the house many times since his death, almost as if he is searching for something.

THE CAPITOL

The oldest building on Commercial Row and the second oldest in town, the capitol was built by William Hurd in 1870. The building was known as Hurd's Saloon, which occupied the first floor. It was on the second floor that Truckee's first district court was convened in 1872. The vigilante group known as the 601 also held meetings here.

The bar witnessed a few skirmishes and gunfights back in the day. Some believe a friendly spirit or two from those early days haunts the building. If I had to guess, I'd say one of the ghosts is that of Constable Jake Teeter, who died here in a gun battle with James Reed on November 7, 1891. Everyone in Truckee knew that Reed and Teeter despised each other. There was little doubt that Teeter had been the aggressor in the fatal shootout. Donner historian Charles Fayette McGlashan defended Reed. The coroner's jury found that, while he had shot and killed the constable, Reed had acted in self-defense. Both Reed and Teeter are buried in the Truckee Cemetery. Apparently, Constable Teeter regrets his decision to provoke James Reed that night. It could be that he haunts the capitol hoping for a do-over.

Many literary and screen notables tossed back a drink at the capitol; among them were John Steinbeck, H.G. Wells, Clark Gable, Buster Keaton and Charlie Chaplin, who some believe haunts the building. Rumor is that he appeared on the stage at the Capitol Theater, located on the second floor of the building.

It's not really such a stretch. Chaplin, who began filming his classic film *The Gold Rush* on February 21, 1924, in the Truckee area, took time from the shooting schedule to explore Truckee. Since silent movies were shown in the theater upstairs, he might well have entertained some of the town's citizens on the small stage between showings.

If he is haunting the place, it could be that he is remembering the romance he had with fifteen-year-old Lita Grey during the filming of *The Gold Rush*. Lita Grey only filmed a few scenes before it was discovered that she was pregnant, forcing the much older Chaplin into a hasty marriage. Georgia Hale replaced Grey in the film. *The Gold Rush* is one of Chaplin's most-loved movies. Is it any wonder then that he might haunt the location where he filmed it?

D.B. Frink and the 601

Truckee was a wild town in its infancy. Lawmen were outnumbered by the dangerous cutthroats who roamed the town's streets, robbing and killing when they saw fit. Seeing the violence happening more frequently, those who wanted law and order did what other towns across the West had done. They formed a secret vigilante committee and called it the 601, like the vigilante committee in Virginia City. Like the vigilantes of the Comstock, the 601 was made up of the town's influential citizens. The name 601 is thought to mean six feet under, zero trials and one rope. Whether or not it actually did mean this is open to interpretation. When the vigilantes wanted to warn a troublemaker to leave town, they hung red ribbons as a warning—leave town or die. Most took heed and skedaddled. Some didn't. One of those who didn't leave was the bad-tempered brothel inmate, Carrie Pryor, aka Spring Chicken. She openly challenged the 601.

Among the members of the vigilante committee was D.B. Frink, the editor and proprietor of the *Truckee Republican* newspaper. Frink took part in rousting Carrie Pryor, but something went terribly wrong that night in November 1874. When the shooting stopped and the smoke cleared, D.B. Frink lay dead on the floor, shot by other members of the secret group. The next day (November 26, 1874), the *Truckee Republican* carried a maudlin story on Frink's untimely death.

"D.B. Frink"

The man whose name heads this column is no longer among the living. It is fitting that some tribute, some testimonial of his worth as a citizen and a man, should be made by the hand of another through the medium by which he attested his devotion to the interests of Truckee. Ever foremost in every measure that promised to give permanence, security and peace to our institutions, it is not strange that his life was yielded up in the endeavor to prove his professions. That there was an entire informality in the manner of his death; that the dread messenger came to him without warning, in the dead of the night, by an unknown hand, does not detract from the effect of his sacrifice. He lies cold in the habiliments of death, a martyr to law and order.

Although the 601 was a secret group, it is apparent that most people in town knew of Frink's involvement with them. During an inquest in the death, several people testified about what happened that fateful night. The verdict of the coroner's jury found that forty-year-old Frink had met death through the hand of an unknown person. And that appears to be the end of it. Still, I can't help but wonder whether D.B. Frink is among the ghosts that haunt Hurd's old saloon at the capitol. It was here that the 601 was formed and where they held their meetings. It may be that Frink wants justice. Perhaps he wants only to question members of the long-ago group in hopes of discovering who was responsible for his death.

RIVER STREET INN

Built in 1882, the River Street Inn is a charming little hotel in central Truckee. Located on the site where the home of the unfortunate Constable Jake Teeter once stood, the inn is haunted by at least one friendly ghost. The unobtrusive ghost is believed to be none other than Mrs. Teeter, who has been seen wandering the hallways and the basement. Those who have encountered the ghostly Mrs. Teeter say that when she speaks she always asks, "Where is Jacob?"

Apparently, she hasn't gotten word that he is over on Front Street, haunting the capitol. It goes well beyond the standard until death to us part. Like a good spouse of long ago, she patiently awaits her husband's return.

GHOSTS OF THE SIERRA SUMMIT

As the California Zephyr train cuts across tracks that follow the same path taken by the Donner Party during their tragic journey, passengers occasionally catch a glimpse of ghostly figures clad in long, white robes that appear on clear, cold winter nights. These specters seem to mournfully point toward a certain area and then vanish as quickly as they came. This is where they met death. For whatever reason, they have chosen to stay here.

When President Abraham Lincoln signed the Pacific Railway Act in 1862, construction of the transcontinental railroad began. For the next six years, jobs on the railroad were plentiful. The work was grueling and dangerous; thousands of Chinese laborers laid track across California and Nevada. All too often, they perished in terrible accidents. More than a dozen men met death on the railroads in this area. One of them was Harry Darraugh, who was crushed between two cars a week before Christmas 1868. Several men died in the wreckage of a train that was derailed in a blinding, heavy winter storm high up on the summit.

STEWART MCKAY'S TOMB

Stewart McKay was a man who knew what he wanted—a tomb of his own, high up in the Sierras above Donner Lake. McKay came to Truckee in 1873, about the same time that Captain Barter perished in Lake Tahoe. For a time,

A summit of the Sierra Nevada—snow sheds in foreground and Donner Lake in the distance. *Photo by Andrew J. Russell. Library of Congress.*

McKay was the owner of the Whitney House, which later would become the Truckee Hotel. In addition to the hotel, he was also a land and sawmill owner. McKay is credited with developing the first tourists' resort camp in the area. As he grew older, the eccentric and wealthy McKay planned for his future by having his final resting place ready and waiting, just as Captain Barter had done. And just as Captain Barter never rested in his tomb, Stewart McKay never rested in his.

As humans, we make plans for the future and hope it will go somewhat as planned, so it was on a morning in 1892 when a reporter from the *San Francisco Morning Call* spoke with Stewart McKay about his tomb. The resulting article, dated August 25, 1892, states:

"No Graveyard for Him"

A Truckee Man's Lone Tomb high the Sierras. HIS VERY ODD EPITAPH. "I Don't Want to Be Woke Up Before Resurrection Day," He Says and the Chances Are In His Favor. "I'm going to be buried in a place where I won't be woke up before resurrection day."

Stewart McKay of Truckee is the man who said talk, and he evidently meant it.

"I've looked all over the country and I can't find a quieter place than that up there," he went on.

It was away up in the high Sierra, looking down on that bluest of blue sheets of water—Donner Lake. Naked peaks rose in awful solemnity and made men seem like the ants are about the only wild game in the neighborhood. Mr. McKay is 55 years of age and he is still in business with the well-known firm of hale and hearty, but while he is uncertain as to whether Ills hotel in Truckee will burn down for the fourth time—he has had three fires already—he knows one thing very thoroughly: Someday he must die. His education on that point worries him more than his algebra or his grammar. It is more trouble to him, in fact, than all his money. McKay has been very wealthy. In the days when John Mackay made his pile McKay had the job of furnishing lumber to the Comstock mines. He is a bachelor and has managed to cling to his ducats about as well as Sierra bachelors generally do, perhaps a little better. He would have been a good deal better off had it not been for those three disastrous fires of his. A Call *reporter who was sent up to view McKay's tomb the other day found it quite stationary. Into the top of a mammoth granite rock McKay has had a stonecutter chisel out a hole big enough to hold six men. "I want plenty of room," he said when he gave the order to the workman. "But four feet will be deep enough, as It's rather hard digging." It was hard digging. If every man who was buried had to be put in such a place as that half the population would have to turn gravediggers. The grave is all dug and nearly ready for McKay's reception, but he says he is going to have the face of the rock dressed up a little, and this inscription will be engraven on the side: Stewart McKay, Resurrection Day.*

It sounded grand as the reporter went on to say how quiet and peaceful the area was. Much of that has changed with the sound of vehicles along Interstate 80 echoing across the mountaintops. It doesn't matter to Stewart McKay. When he died in 1917, his body was cremated and the ashes were tossed in the Truckee Cemetery. So much for all those plans, but this isn't to say that no one was able to enjoy McKay's tomb. According to a friend who grew up in Truckee, the tomb was once a favorite hangout of the local teenagers. I wonder if any of them ever encountered the ghost of Stewart McKay as he wandered along the tomb. Perhaps some of those who visit the tomb might change their minds about doing so if they knew about the ghostly McKay. I won't mention the specter if you won't.

China Cove, Donner Lake

Ghostly figures are also seen at Donner Lake. Their pitiful moans are said to echo across the tall pine trees on moonless winter nights. The victims of greed and betrayal, they rest uneasy.

Located in the town of Truckee, Donner Lake is about eleven miles northwest of Lake Tahoe. Much smaller than and not nearly as deep as Lake Tahoe, Donner Lake is a favorite with fisherman. Some of the largest lake trout in the state of California are found in its waters. When the ill-fated Donner Party was stranded nearby in the winter of 1847, the lake was known as Truckee Lake. But like the nearby pass and summit, the lake was renamed after the Donner Party.

Aside from the unfathomable cannibalism committed by some members of the Donner Party, there is the dark story at China Cove about the bones of hundreds of Chinese laborers resting at the bottom of Donner Lake. The victims of railroad accidents and of unscrupulous people, they were among the thousands of Chinese who came to California during the gold rush and stayed on to work on the railroad.

In 1867, more than ten thousand Chinese laborers were brought to the region to work on the transcontinental railroad. Many Chinese settled in Truckee, built their own neighborhoods and kept to themselves. As in other parts of the United States, the Chinese faced racism and prejudice here. When much of Truckee's Chinatown was burned down in the 1870s, whites tore down the remaining buildings and gave the Chinese one week to leave town. They did. The new Chinese neighborhood was built just outside of town.

Donner Lake in the Sierra Nevada as seen from Donner Pass in July 2013. *Photo by Frank Schulenburg.*

Racism against them continued decades after the railroad was completed in 1869. In 1882, President Chester A. Arthur signed the Chinese Exclusion Act, which severely limited Chinese immigration into the United States. The act was not repealed until 1943.

According to author Sylvia Sun Minnick in her book *Chinese Funeral Customs*, although they came to this country to build new lives, the Chinese—especially the Cantonese from Kwantung Province—wanted their remains returned home and buried in China. Sun Minnick states, "Chinese feared that when they died their spirits would not rest until their remains were in a proper grave at home."

This was in accordance with the Chinese proverb, "If anyone obtains honor and wealth, and never returns to his home, he is a well-dressed person walking in the dark."

No one wanted a restless ghost to walk in the darkness. In 1864, Mark Twain wrote of the Chinese custom of bones being taken to China for reburial:

> *On the Pacific coast the Chinamen all belong to one or another of several great companies or organizations, and these companies keep track of their members, register their names, and ship their bodies home when they die. The See Yup Company is held to be the largest of these. The Ning Yeong Company is next, and numbers eighteen thousand members on the coast. Its headquarters are at San Francisco, where it has a costly temple, several great officers…and numerous priesthood. In it I was shown a register of its members, with the dead and the date of their shipment to China duly marked. Every ship that sails from San Francisco carries away a heavy freight of Chinese corpses—or did, at least, until the [California State] legislature, with an ingenious refinement of Christian cruelty, forbade the shipments, as a neat underhanded way of deterring Chinese immigration. The bill was offered, whether it passed or not. It is my impression that it passed.*

Preparation and shipment of the remains was costly. While they may have paid others well to disinter their remains, scrape the bones clean and pack them for shipment back to China, this didn't always happen. Instead, according to some stories, the remains were haplessly dumped wherever it was convenient. This happened to be at China Cove in Donner Lake. Another tale has the Chinese laborers being given the most dangerous work on the railroad. If they died while working, their bodies were unceremoniously tossed into Donner Lake. Some say this is why so many ghosts haunt Donner Lake.

SPRING CHICKEN AND THE RED-LIGHT LADIES

It's rumored that more than one ghostly red-light lady walks Jibboom Street. Jibboom Street, Truckee's red-light district, was dotted with brothels and saloons. This rough area where every vice flourished was said to be the largest red-light district in the West. Businesses along Front Street had back doors so that their customers could go to Jibboom Street (referred to as the back street) and return without much notice.

The young women who plied their trade here were frequently addicted to drugs and alcohol. They lived hopelessly hard and violent lives. Rarely did such a woman successfully climb out of the gutter she had fallen into. All too often, suicide was her only escape.

One of the many to die by her own hand was nineteen-year-old Alice Taffe. The *Truckee Republican* reported on Taffe's death in the November 1, 1876 issue:

"Suicide"

On Monday evening last, about ten 'o'clock [sic] *Alice Taffe, a fast woman and a resident of Mrs. M. Hall's dance house on the back street, committed suicide by taking morphine.*

Nineteen-year-old Alice Taffe and her friend Annie Starr went to the bar of Hall's dance house. There, she noticed an old boyfriend and asked him to dance with her. When he refused to dance, Alice and Annie left the bar only to return a short while later. In her hand, Alice had a paper wrapper marked poison.

"I'm going to die. I've taken morphine. And this will be the end of it," Alice said to Mrs. Hall.

Mrs. Hall didn't pay much attention. Such threats were always being made by one girl or another. Suddenly, Alice fell against the bar and was taken upstairs and put in bed to sleep it off. When she started foaming at the mouth, they realized that Alice had really poisoned herself. Dr. Curless was sent for, but there was nothing he could do. She lingered on another two hours. The newspaper summed up her death thus:

It is hard to conjecture what activated her in committing the rash deed but jealousy was probably the cause. It is easy to understand how these poor, degraded outcasts, when in their sense, when they take a retrospective view of their lives,—what they are and what they might have been are desperate enough to take their own lives.

Another such outcast and denizen of Truckee's red-light district was Carrie Pryor Smith, also known as Spring Chicken. The idiom "spring chicken" has been used to refer to a young woman since the 1700s and may be the origin of Smith's moniker.

Her downfall wasn't drugs or alcohol but her hot temper. She couldn't stay out of trouble, no matter how she tried or where she went. While in Virginia City, she was arrested and put in jail. The infamous soiled dove wanted out, but she thought of death as that way out. So she tried to commit suicide, first by morphine and then by hanging herself. Both attempts failed. When she was set free, her antics continued. Although prostitutes were not permitted to enter the businesses along Front Street, there were no rules about them fighting there. On July 4, 1877, Carrie Pryor Smith and Lotta Morton had a shootout on the street. Carrie escaped Lotta's bullets; unfortunately, Lotta wasn't so lucky. In condemning Carrie, the July 4, 1877 *Truckee Republican* characterized her as having led "a most dissolute, abandoned life and has been the direct and immediate cause of several homicides. Her own fair hand has more than once been dyed with human blood."

While many of the lonely specters of red-light ladies are content to stay in and around Jibboom Street, Carrie Pryor Smith is not. She is the woman known to haunt several businesses on Front Street. This could be a case of a ghost having more freedom in death than was afforded her in life. Those who have seen Carrie's specter describe her as being elegantly attired, with her hair swept up into a fashionable topknot and smiling demurely. Perhaps death has given her a better fashion sense and taken the edge off her terrible temper.

SUICIDE BY CHAINSAW

On August 15, 1906 Charles A. Teeter cut his own throat and subsequently bled to death. Certainly, it was a horrible way to go, but Teeter's suicide pales in comparison to that of Richard Possehl. His was the first recorded suicide by chainsaw in the United States and the second in the world. What a horrendous way to die—slitting one's throat with a chainsaw. But this is exactly what tree trimmer Richard Possehl did on June 27, 1993. When the twenty-seven-year-old's body was found lying beside his pickup near the Truckee Cemetery, the Nevada County Sheriff's Department began investigating the death as a homicide. What else could it be? Was it even possible to commit suicide in such a way?

When it was discovered that only Possehl's fingerprints were found on the equipment, the investigation changed. And after extensive tests in which a mannequin was used to stand in for Possehl, it was determined that the unemployed Possehl had indeed slit his own throat and nearly severed his head using a chainsaw.

Suicide can sometimes lead to a haunting, as can a violent death. Perhaps this is why, although he is buried across the country in Minnesota, Possehl's ghost is believed to haunt the area near the cemetery. Witnesses have described the specter as angry and confused.

Rocking Stone

Often associated with witchcraft, rocking stones are found throughout the world. Truckee's famous rocking stone is a seventeen-ton boulder that the Washoe tribe held sacred. On it, their fish and dried meat were kept safe from birds and animals. Donner historian and attorney Charles Fayette McGlashan built his family mansion near the stone. In 1935, the home burned to the ground, but the rocking stone remained. One touch of the finger, and the boulder would move.

Although it has long since been cemented into place, the rocking stone is still a popular attraction in Truckee. And the ghost that lingers nearby? No one is positive who she is, only that the glowing lady is known to occasionally appear at this location.

Mary and the Ghosts of Rainbow Lodge

A few years ago, a young couple on my Reno ghost walk showed me a remarkable photo they had captured at Rainbow Lodge. The photo was taken on one of their cellphones and appeared to be a somewhat smoky outline of a woman.

"That's her! That's Mary the ghost," the man exclaimed. "Can you see her?"

I could. "I'd love to have a copy of this," I told them. After agreeing to send me one, they went on their way. I never did get that photograph, nor did I expect to. People lose cellphones and interest, and sometimes they forget. It is what it is, folks. So the ghostly Mary and her photo were pushed to the back of my mind. They stayed there until I started working on this book, and my author friend Richard Senate shared his Truckee notes with me. Ah, Mary. I remembered her and that photo—now I had to find out more.

Rainbow Lodge near Cisco Grove and Donner Pass Road on the Yuba River was built in the early 1900s and may have been quite a chichi place (in a log-hewn sort of way) for the après ski set. I can see it in the pre-drought days—snow falling and quickly piling up as skiers in Nordic sweaters sat around a roaring fire, sipping hot chocolate or brandy. Thirty rooms were available, give or take, at the expanded Rainbow Lodge. That was a lot of skiers. But long before the skiers and the hot cocoa, this was a popular stage stop that was actually established in the late 1800s. As a matter of fact, the Rainbow Lodge sits on a section of the old Emigrant Trail.

And now we come to the ghost of Mary. While she is not the only ghost in residence, she is the spirit that seems to want to interact the most with the living. She is not mean or malicious but will try all manner of attention-seeking antics—from turning lights off and on to pinching someone's arm. There are two stories as to how Mary became a ghost. The first has her husband finding her in bed with another man. Furious at her betrayal, he shot and killed both Mary and her lover. In the alternative story, Mary was innocent of adultery and was merely the victim of an insanely jealous spouse. Either way, she haunts the Rainbow Lodge to this day. While Mary prefers room twenty-three, her erstwhile lover (or friend) moves about from room to room. The sound of weeping that echoes through the lodge from time to time is thought to be Mary, regretting the behavior that led to her death—or not.

There is also the tale of a gambler who was murdered here when it was discovered he had several aces up his sleeve. He's been seen wandering the dining area only to vanish the moment someone spots him. The Rainbow Lodge is a great place to spend the night or grab a meal, but don't deal the gambling ghost in—remember, he cheats.

4

THE DONNER PARTY

DONNER PARTY TRAGEDY

Indeed, if I do not experience something far worse than I have yet done, I shall say the trouble is all in getting started.
—Tamsen Donner, June 1846

When the young wife and mother wrote these cheery words, she could not have known what horror awaited her in the high Sierras. She could not have known that half of those who started this journey would meet death along the way or that those who survived would be forced to eat the dead just to stay alive.

In the spring of 1846, eighty-seven men, women and children left Independence, Missouri, and headed for California. Within two years, a discovery at Sutter's Fort would mark the beginning of the California gold rush; gold would be the impetus for the western migration of thousands. On this morning in April 1846, however, the families who joined the trek westward did so in hope of a better life.

As the wagon train moved slowly westward, it was plagued by one mishap after another. There would be deaths and killings and, finally, the fateful decision that led them to disaster.

After consulting Lansford Hastings's book *Emigrants' Guide to Oregon and California*, Donner Party leaders decided to save time by taking what was called the Hastings Cutoff. Even though Lansford Hastings himself had never taken his suggested route and experienced travelers warned against it, their minds were made up.

By the time the Donner Party reached present-day Reno, they'd been beset with bad luck and problems. The Hastings Cutoff had cost them precious time, and they were smaller in numbers. Death claimed an elderly woman during the first weeks of their journey. James Reed, the wealthiest member of the party, had been banished for killing another man. When an elderly man couldn't keep up, he was abandoned on the trail and left to die in the desert. Illness claimed a young man in the salt flats. Murder and accident took two more lives.

While the party camped in present-day Reno, they may have thought trouble was behind them. It was late October. The weather was balmy, and there was plenty of water and green grass in the distant Sierras. Leaders were urged to move the party westward; the weather in the Sierras could change in an instant, especially this late in the season. Just as they had with the Hastings Cutoff, the leaders ignored the warnings. They were exhausted and needed rest.

Finally, they pulled up stakes and headed west on the last leg of their long journey. A major storm was forming off the coast of California. By the time the Donner Party reached present-day Verdi (ten miles west), the air had turned icy, and snow had begun to fall. A fierce wind blew down from the Sierras, churning the snow into a white fury. As they slowly moved forward, the snow fell heavier. George Donner's lead wagon was forced to stop because of a broken axle. As he desperately tried to make repairs, his hand slipped on the jagged edge of wood. Ignoring the nasty gash, Donner told the others to continue on. He and Tamsen and their family would stay where they were until the storm passed. They encamped at Alder Creek in hastily constructed shelters as the other wagons slowly rolled onward in the snow.

The others only made it six miles from the Donners' encampment before they, too, were forced to stop in the heavy snow. They were stuck. It was impossible to move forward in the blizzard, and there was no retreat to the meadows in the east. They would stay there until the snow stopped falling. Crawling out of the wagons, men and women claimed locations where their families would wait. For their residence, the Breen family chose an abandoned cabin that Moses Schallenberger had lived in the previous year. Louis and Philippine Keseberg and their children resided in a lean-to that backed to the Breen cabin. The Murphys built a shelter against a large boulder nearby. Mrs. Reed, whose husband had

A walking trail near the Murphy cabin site of the Donner tragedy. *Photo by Bill Oberding.*

been banished, was in a small shelter with her children. None of them had ever experienced weather like this before nor were they prepared for the freezing winds that blew across the treetops, piling the snow in drifts taller than a man. They lit fires and ate their evening meals, and then huddled in delicately stitched quilts and told themselves that surely the storm would let up in a few days. It didn't.

The days wore on. Before long, the meager food supply dwindled. Faced with starvation and certain death, some of those trapped in the two high Sierras camps began to eye the dead hungrily. After they had consumed livestock, pet dogs, tree branches and broth made of boiled leather, they resorted to cannibalism.

Some view Tamsen Donner as the heroine of the Donner Party. Much mystery and speculation surround this educated woman who had started westward with her second husband, her children and such high hopes. When rescuers finally arrived at Alder Creek that spring, Tamsen Donner refused go with them. She adamantly refused to leave her dying husband's side, even though staying meant certain death.

Stumps of trees cut by the Donner Party in Summit Valley, Placer County. *Library of Congress.*

She willingly sent her children on with rescuers but stayed behind with her husband at Alder Creek. After his death, she walked the six miles to the Lake Camp and found Louis Keseberg, who had been forced to stay behind because of a foot injury. What happened afterward is shrouded in mystery. When rescuers returned, Tamsen Donner was dead.

Louis Keseberg said that Donner arrived at his cabin one evening soaking wet and shivering. He offered her something to eat, but she refused to partake of human flesh. Rambling incoherently about going to her children, Tamsen Donner had lain down on a bed of rags and fell asleep. The next morning, according to Keseberg, she was dead. Her body was never recovered, and when rescuers arrived, he readily admitted to cannibalizing her. According to some, he claimed her body had rendered five pounds of fat. Others said he'd actually bragged that Tamsen Donner's was the tastiest flesh he'd ever consumed.

True or not, these stories and others gave rise to the belief that he killed the unfortunate woman for her flesh and her money. The stigma followed Louis Keseberg for the rest of his days, but not everyone believed him a killer.

In 1911, Tamsen Donner's youngest daughter, Eliza P. Donner Houghton, published *The Expedition of the Donner Party and Its Tragic Fate*. In the book, Houghton told of her visit to Louis Keseberg in 1879. When she asked him to tell her the truth about her mother's death, he said:

> *On my knees before you, and in the sight of God, I want to assert my innocence. Mrs. Houghton, if I had murdered your mother, would I stand here with my hand between your hands, look into your pale face, see the tear-marks on your cheeks, and the quiver of your lips as you ask the question? No, God Almighty is my witness, I am innocent of your mother's death.*

Houghton believed him.

The rock that formed the fireplace of the Murphy cabin bears the memorial plaque. *Photo by Bill Oberding.*

Tall pine trees at Donner State Park. *Photo by Bill Oberding.*

A close-up of plaque bearing the names of members of the Donner Party, those who survived and perished in the tragedy. *Photo by Bill Oberding.*

When a tragedy of this magnitude occurs, it probably changes the essence of a location forever. This is why some who visit Donner Memorial State Park report strong feelings of negativity and sadness. Years ago, I took a visiting relative to the site. We spent an hour or so in the Emigrant Trail Museum before walking the trail. During this time, she didn't say one word. But later, as we drove back to Reno, she said, "I could never go back there. There's just too much—too much pain—too much negativity hanging in the air."

Although I regularly visit the park a couple times a year, I understood what she meant. It is palpable, and if you're the least bit sensitive, you can feel it.

Donner Memorial State Park is located off Interstate 80 approximately ten miles from Lake Tahoe. With several campsites, the Emigrant Trail Museum and a walking trail, the park is a popular spot with tourists and locals. There are those who believe this park and nearby Alder Creek are haunted by members of the tragic Donner Party.

A ghostly Tamsen Donner is said to walk the area late at night, and a middle-aged man dressed in the attire of 150 years ago has been sighted in the museum many times.

When paranormal investigators recently visited the museum, there were some in the group who felt a strong presence near the wagon display.

The names of every Donner Party member are inscribed on the plaque that is attached to the Murphy cabin rock. The bodies of those who perished here were said to have been buried in a common grave near this rock. Others believe they were actually buried closer to the site of Pioneer Memorial rock. Strong electromagnetic field detector readings have been reported in both areas, and EVP has been obtained near the rock and the Pioneer Monument.

Alder Creek, the site of the George Donner family encampment, is a popular day-use facility approximately six miles from Donner Memorial State Park. Near the trail's halfway point is a tree that is identified as the location of the Donner shelters. However, there is some doubt among historians and other researchers as to the actual location. Some believe that it is beneath the waters of Prosser Reservoir; others think it is in the meadows closer to the creek.

Recent archaeological excavations have been conducted at Alder Creek. Perhaps those findings will not only give us the precise location but also answer other questions pertaining to the tragedy that occurred here in the winter of 1846 and spring of 1847.

LOUIS KESEBERG

Did He or Didn't He

Did Louis Keseberg kill Tamsen Donner? The debate continues, with many historians agreeing that he was indeed Donner's killer. Rescuers said that when they left her, Donner was healthy and in the possession of gold coins.

While the other Donner Party survivors were eventually able to go on with their lives, Louis Keseberg could not. When rescuer Edward Coffeemeyer arrived at Sutter's Fort with horrendous tales of Keseberg's having murdered Tamsen Donner for her money and to satisfy his taste for human flesh, most people believed every word of it. Keseberg filed suit for slander against Coffeemeyer and won. His award was the princely sum of one dollar. This didn't stop him from being vilified as a murder and a cannibal.

A walking trail at Donner Memorial State Park. *Photo by Bill Oberding.*

A popular myth has Keseberg opening a restaurant in Sacramento in later years. While it sounds deliciously gruesome, it didn't happen. He managed a hotel and ran a brewery. But did he kill Tamsen Donner? I don't know.

Keseberg was young, only thirty-two years old at the time of the Donner tragedy. The ghostly bearded old man that's been spotted in and around the Donner campsite may well be Keseberg's specter, but this is not how he would have appeared when he was stranded near Truckee (Donner) Lake.

CAMP OUT AT DONNER MEMORIAL STATE PARK

I'm not much of an outdoors person, but the prospect of camping where the Donner Party did appealed to my quirky sense of fun. And what if—yes, just suppose that a ghost of one of them might make its way into our tent and give us a firsthand account of the tragedy. My choice for that was Tamsen Donner. After all, she is the ghost that people usually encounter here. So we packed up the car and headed west on Interstate 80. The plan was to meet some ghost-hunting friends at the park.

On a warm late-summer day, we selected our campsite and proceeded to settle in. Recording EVP would be difficult here. Unlike the silence the Donner Party encountered, this is a noisy place with the cars continually speeding by on the interstate. But then again, this might provide the perfect white noise we would need to get something good. While it was still daylight we walked to the monument where the remains of those who perished are said to be buried. A psychic with us said, "No…no bodies were ever here."

So we walked to the rock that formed the fireplace for the Murphy cabin. The rock bears a plaque with the names of those who died and those who survived.

"I hear horses," the psychic said, "many horses."

She stood in deep thought, "This is where they buried the remains."

With darkness came the flying bugs, and the noises of creatures that wandered through the site once the sun set. After a hasty hotdog barbecue, we were off. Armed with flashlights, cameras, dowsing rods and recorders, we

A Donner Memorial State Park sign. *Photo by Bill Oberding.*

made our way along the trail, calling the names of those who had perished there. "Tamsen Donner, do you hear us? What about you, Mr. Wolfinger, Jay Fosdick and Eleanor Eddy, are you here?"

We couldn't remember all their names; forty-one people died here and were devoured by those who survived. So our next question, "Do you know what happened to your body after you died?"

Yes, that might have been a dumb question to ask, but it's always good to know what frame of mind a ghost is in.

The cars continued to race by on the highway. A chill hung in the air; summer or not, it gets cold here as night wears on. Back at our tents, we listened to our recordings. To the question "Do you know what happened to your body after you died?" There was a faint response: "Lies."

Did this mean cannibalization didn't take place here or did it mean someone lied to someone else?

Late that night came the real test. I knew the park was haunted. How could it not be, considering what happened here? Ghosts are OK, but bears—now that's something different entirely. What if an angry bear tore into our tent? It could happen. Bears do live in the Truckee/Tahoe area. And they weren't hibernating. Then, I asked myself, what about mountain lions? They are ferocious, too. I would never want to kill an animal, nor would I want an animal killing me. Ghosts are another matter. We could come back some night and not spend the night. Yes, that sounded like a great idea. I woke my husband. "It's 2:30 in the morning, I can't sleep. Do you want to go home?" I asked.

He knew the drill. He's camped with me before. We packed up, left a note for our friends, bid the ghosts and all the animals goodbye and headed to the warmth of home. Camping, like ghost hunting, isn't for everyone.

To Cannibalize or Not

The mystery of what actually happened during the winter of 1846 will likely never be solved, certainly not to everyone's satisfaction. Did the members of the Donner Party actually cannibalize the bodies of those who perished? I think they did. This, I believe, is one reason for all the ghostly activity and the aura that hangs over the Donner Park area to this very day. It is an aura of heartache, suffering and desperation. On certain days (and nights), you can feel it more intensely. Probably not everyone resorted to cannibalism, but mothers who refused to eat the flesh of others probably served it up to their children in an effort to save their lives.

Some disagree with me, and that is OK. There have been hundreds of books written about the Donner Party. Some claim that cannibalism was a fact at the ill-fated camp; others put it in the legend category. However, the diary of Donner Party member Patrick Breen makes it obvious that cannibalism did occur here. The February 26, 1847 entry states:

Frid 26th

Froze hard last night to day clear & warm Wind S.E. blowing briskly. Martha's jaw swelled with the toothache: hungry times in camp; plenty hides, but the folks will not eat them. We eat them with a tolerable good apetite. Thanks be to Almighty God. Amen. Mrs. Murphy said here yesterday that [she] *thought she would Commence on Milt. & eat him. I don't* [think] *that she has done so yet; it is distressing. The Donners, 4 days ago, told the California folks that they* [would] *commence to eat the dead people if they did not succeed, that day or next, in finding their cattle,* [which were] *then under ten or twelve feet of snow, &* [the Donners] *did not know the spot or near it; I suppose they have done so ere this time.*

Yes, I suppose they did as well. Here, I will tell you about a very strange incident that happened to me several years ago after visiting the Donner Memorial State Park.

It was early fall and still warm. A friend and I drove out the Donner site one evening to look around. With flashlights in hand, we made our way toward the memorial rock and around the walking trail. Being a psychic, she picked up many spirits entrenched at the location. While some were confused and unhappy, most of them were relieved that they had moved beyond this life; they didn't want to go anywhere else and were content to stay in the area. We attempted EVP, but due to the noise of cars on nearby Highway 80, we didn't succeed. As the evening wore on, a distinct chill fell across the park, and not dressed for it, we made our way back to the car.

As she drove us back to Reno, I talked about what the Donners must have endured. "It just makes you feel so sad to think about it when right down the street is a Burger King," I joked.

No sooner were the words out of my mouth than they were repeated in a mocking tone—from the backseat of the car. There were only two of us in the vehicle, and my friend was not a ventriloquist. So what logical explanation was there? We decided a Donner Party ghost had come along with us and was playing a joke on us. Neither of us said another word until we got to my house. There, we told the ghost that he was not welcome and had two choices: return to the park or go into the light. I assume that he chose to go back to the park. I've never heard another word from him.

DONNER PARTY CHRONICLER

With his coverage of Utah's Mountain Meadows Massacre, Truckee historian, newspaper editor and attorney Charles Fayette McGlashan achieved a certain amount of notoriety. But when a surviving member of the Donner Party subscribed to the *Truckee Republican*, McGlashan's curiosity was peaked. A correspondence was begun, as well as a series of articles on the plight of the Donner Party. This led to work on his book entitled *History of the Donner Party*. While conducting his research, McGlashan, who lived three miles away from the camp site, spent time in the area of the tragic encampment, interviewed several survivors and collected Donner Party relics. An interesting outcome of McGlashan's research was the meeting he arranged between Tamsen Donner's youngest daughter, Eliza Houghton, and Louis Keseberg, Tamsen's suspected killer.

McGlashan later wrote the following concerning that meeting:

> *Keseberg said, "Mr. McGlashan has told me you have questions about what happened in the mountain cabin and you want to ask me yourself."*
>
> *"Yes, for the eye of God and your eyes witnessed my mother's last hours, and I have come to ask you, in the presence of that Other Witness, when, where, and how she died," Eliza asked.*
>
> *Keseberg dropped to his knees and said, "On my knees before you, and in the sight of God, I want to assert my innocence."*
>
> *Eliza took the elderly man's hand in hers and said, "Now speak, Mr. Keseberg, with your hand in mine."*
>
> *"I did not kill your mother, or harm her in any way," Keseberg said, staring Eliza squarely in the eyes.*
>
> *Eliza accepted his words as truth.*

In his 1879 *History of the Donner Party*, McGlashan wrote of how the rescue party disposed of the bodies:

General Kearney visited the cabins at Donner Lake on the twenty-second of June, 1847. Edwin Bryant, the author of "What I Saw in California," was with General Kearney, and says: "A halt was ordered for the purpose of collecting and interring the remains. Near the principal cabins I saw two bodies entire, with the exception that the abdomens had been cut open and the entrails extracted. Their flesh had been either wasted by famine or evaporated by exposure to the dry atmosphere, and they presented the appearance of mummies. Strewn around the cabins were dislocated and broken skulls (in some instances sawed asunder with care, for the purpose of extracting the brains), human skeletons, in short, in every variety of mutilation. A more revolting and appalling spectacle I never witnessed. The remains were, by an order of General Kearney, collected and buried under the superintendence of Major Swords. They were interred in a pit which had been dug in the center of one of the cabins for a cache. These melancholy duties to the dead being performed, the cabins, by order of Major Swords, were fired, and with everything surrounding them connected with this horrid and melancholy tragedy were consumed. The body of George Donner was found at his camp, about eight or ten miles distant, wrapped in a sheet. He was buried by a party of men detailed for that purpose.

According to some of the rescuers, the remains of those who perished in the Donner tragedy were buried beneath this rock. *Photo by Bill Oberding.*

His book was well received, immediately capturing the public's interest, but Charles Fayette McGlashan was far from finished with his work. He had long believed that a memorial should be built in honor of all those who had perished in that terrible winter of 1846–47. For that, he would have to wait several years.

THE DONNER TREASURE

On Saturday morning, May 16, 1891, the following article appeared in the *Sacramento Record-Union*:

> *TRUCKEE. May 15 Truckee is feverish with excitement over the discovery of a portion of the treasure buried by the Donner Party in 1846–47. There is no doubt about the authenticity of the find or the identity of the money.*
>
> *McGlashan's* History of the Donner Party, *in speaking of the second relief party, says: "Reed's party encamped the first night near the upper end of Donner Lake. They had scarcely traveled three miles upon starting from the Graves cabin. Mrs. Graves had taken with her a considerable sum of money. This money had been ingeniously concealed in augur holes bored in cleats nailed to the bed of the wagon. These cleats, W.C. Graves says, were ostensibly placed in the wagon-bed to support a table carried in the back part of the wagon. On the underside of these cleats, however, were the augur holes, carefully filled with coin. The sum is variously stated at from $300 to $500.*
>
> *At the camping-ground near the upper end of Donner Lake one of the relief party jokingly proposed to another to play a game of enchre, to see who should have Mrs. Graves' money. Next morning Mrs. Graves remained when the party started, and concealed her money. All that is known is that she buried it behind a large rock on the north side of Donner Lake. So far as is known this money has never been recovered, but still lies hidden where it was placed by Mrs. Graves.*
>
> *The history proceeds to recount the death of Mrs. Graves from cold and starvation three days afterwards. She buried the money on the morning of March 3, 1847, and it was found yesterday afternoon by Edward Reynolds.*
>
> *Stewart McKay employed Amos Lane, keeper of a livery stable, to take him to the upper end of Donner Lake yesterday afternoon. A commercial traveler by the name of Huntsman went as far as Johnson's Resort with them,*

and then took a boat and went out on the lake fishing. This left an empty seat in the wagon at starting, and Lane asked his friend Reynolds to go along.

Reynolds is a stranger in Truckee, having come from Sierra Valley last Tuesday. He is a miner, and instead of going fishing, he went up on the side of the hill to look for quartz.

Meantime Lane and McKay had driven on toward the head of the lake. Reynolds' attention was accidentally called to some dark-looking pieces of money lying in plain sight on top of the ground. Stooping down he picked up ten ancient-looking dollars, and upon scratching slightly in the earth uncovering a large quantity of silver. Not knowing the nature or extent of the deposit he prudently covered it up, and when Lane returned reported that he had found the buried treasure, and offered to take Lane in with him.

It was resolved to drive back to Truckee with McKay and the drummer without disclosing the secret, and to return after dark and dig up the money. Their anxiety finally overcame their discretion, however, and about 3 o'clock they started back to get the plant, taking with them a pick, shovel and two barley sacks to hold the coin.

They found the silver scattered over quite a surface ground, and by the side of the stone, in the place where Reynolds had uncovered the main deposit they found a hatful of coins. Darkness coming on, they returned to town.

On examining the money closely it was all found to be ancient, and all more or less blackened, stained or oxidized, according to the position in which it was found. Suspecting that they had found some of the Donner Party money, they took Stewart McKay and C.F. McGlashan into their secret. They had found $146 in silver, and a number of pieces were of more recent date than 1845.

This morning they returned to the lake, taking Stewart McKay, C.F. McGlashan and Mrs. Nora McGlashan along as witnesses and experts. In one hour the party found $9. Several pieces were firmly imbedded in earth, while others lay loosely on the surface. A large pine tree had been felled directly across the original plant, and it is evident that when the saw logs made from the tree were snaked away they tore up the ground and carried the money along with them for a number of feet.

Logs and wood have been cut all around the spot, and probably a thousand men have passed over the money since the days when the railroad was built.

The place is in plain sight from the wagon road, about 400 feet from the margin of the central part of the lake, opposite the fishing resort of Johnson.

The Donner Monument dedication ceremony, June 6, 1918. *Courtesy of the Emigrant Trail Museum.*

VIRILE TO RISK AND
FIND; KINDLY WITHAL
AND A READY HELP.
FACING THE BRUNT
OF FATE; INDOMI-
TABLE — UNAFRAID.

© 1918
by E. Hess

THE PIONEER MONUMENT
AT DONNER LAKE

A close-up of the Donner Monument dedication ceremony, June 6, 1918. *Left to right*: Nevada governor E.D. Boyle; Donner survivors Martha (Patty Reed) Lewis, Eliza Donner Houghton and Frances Donner Wilder; and California governor W.D. Stephens. *Courtesy of the Emigrant Trail Museum.*

When it was learned that the money was widely scattered and that it would take days and perhaps weeks to find it all, Messrs. Land and Reynolds erected a tent over the spot and had it enclosed with a fence. Guards are stationed on the ground to protect the buried treasure it still contains.

Some authorities place the amount of money buried by the Donner party at $10,000, and searching parties are already being organized to make a systematic hunt for the long hidden coin. From the present indications the hills on the north side of Donner Lake will be covered with treasure hunters tomorrow.

Reynolds and Lane will have the money on exhibition at their tent while continuing their part of the search.

The money they found would delight the heart of a numismatist. There are old, antiquated coins of all dates prior to 1845, and of the most obsolete and forgotten marking. Coins from France, Spain, Bolivia, the Argentine Republic, and a number of other foreign countries besides. A very rare collection of American pieces are in included in the treasure trove. As relics of the Donner party the find is very valuable, one hundred dollars having been offered for one of the pieces. A Truckee hotelkeeper offered ten dollars a day to have the coins placed on exhibition at his hotel. No arrangements will be made regarding he disposition of the money until it is known how much can be found.

On June 6, 1918, the Donner Memorial was unveiled in the presence of many dignitaries, including Charles Fayette McGlashan; California governor W.D. Stevens; Nevada governor E.D. Boyle; and Donner Party survivors Eliza Donner Houghton, Francis Donner Wilder and Martha (Patty Reed) Lewis.

It must have been a bittersweet day of disappointment for McGlashan, who had donated the very land that the memorial was erected on. He believed the memorial stood directly on the site of the Breen cabin, but the official plaque said otherwise. His attempts at having the descriptive wording changed were futile.

The memorial he had fought so hard for now stood in dedication to all emigrants who had forged westward, not exclusively the Donner Party, as McGlashan wanted.

AFTERWORD

I've written this book from the perspective of a historian who believes that ghosts (specters, spirits, phantoms, etc.) do indeed exist. As far as proof positive goes, it's likely we will never answer the question of whether or not ghosts exist to everyone's satisfaction. Still, one thing is certain: when we have run out of logical explanations, we are left with the inexplicable. This is where ghosts, specters, spirits and everything else that goes bump in the night come in. The ghosts I've presented here are no different than those of other regions; they are part of our shared human experience. They bring our deepest fears to light, while reminding us that life, unlike the old 1931 song that claims so, is not always a bowl of cherries. The injustices of life (real or perceived) often give rise to ghosts and hauntings. It is through the very idea of ghosts—their experiences and stories—that we can come to understand that death might not be the end.

Death is the unknown, and there is always something frightening in the unknown. Perhaps ghosts are part of our shared human experience because they make death more comprehensible and, thus, less frightening. I am a ghost investigator and have seen and experienced things that defy explanation. I long ago gave up trying to explain the phenomena of ghosts. Instead, I've decided to enjoy the adventure of ghost research and of ghost investigating. I've shared some of the Tahoe region's legends and my own experiences and encounters with the unknown, as well as those of others. To those who would say these are outrageous and impossible, I will remind that not so many decades ago, organ transplants, cellphones and handheld computers were the stuff of science fiction.

Every day, we learn more about ourselves and the world around us. We may agree on some points of ghosts, history and hauntings while disagreeing on others. In the end, there are more theories in the field of ghost research and investigation than there are answers. Whatever your opinion of ghostly matters is, I truly hope that you've enjoyed reading *Haunted Lake Tahoe* as much as I've enjoyed writing it.

INDEX

V

Virginia City 26, 79, 80, 81, 91, 98
Vive les Girls 39

W

Wilbur Clark's Desert Inn 51
Wright, William 26

ABOUT THE AUTHOR

 An independent historian, Janice plans to return as a docent at the Nevada Historical Society. She is a past docent of the Fourth Ward School Museum in Virginia City. The author of numerous books on Nevada's history, true crime, unusual occurrences and hauntings, she speaks on these subjects throughout the state. Her Ghosthunting 101 and Nevada's Quirky Historical Facts community education classes at Truckee Meadows Community College have been well received.